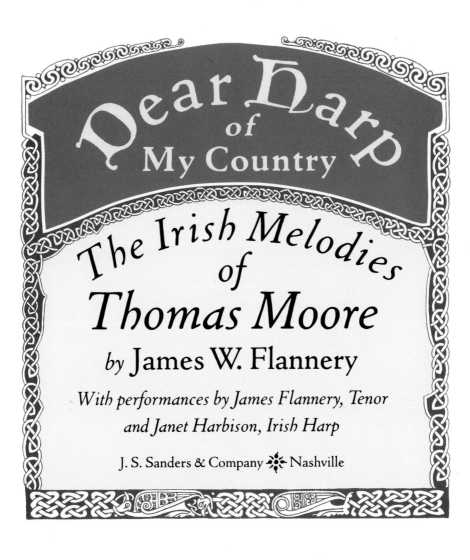

Dear Harp
of
My Country

The Irish Melodies
of
Thomas Moore

by James W. Flannery

With performances by James Flannery, Tenor
and Janet Harbison, Irish Harp

J. S. Sanders & Company ❖ Nashville

Published in the United States by J. S. Sanders & Company
P.O. Box 50331, Nashville, Tennessee 37205   [615] 790-8951

Distributed to the book trade by National Book Network

LIBRARY OF CONGRESS CATALOGING-IN-PUBLICATION DATA

Flannery, James W.
    Dear harp of my country : the Irish melodies of Thomas Moore /
James W. Flannery. — 1st ed.
        p.   cm. — (The spirit of Ireland in lyric and song ; v. 1)
    Includes bibliographical references.
    ISBN 1-879941-36-8 (trade paper)
    1. Moore, Thomas, 1779–1852. Irish melodies.   I. Title.
II. Series.
ML410.M7756F68   1997
782.42'09415—dc21   97-21925
                                                              CIP
                                                              MN

COVER: Detail from *The Marriage of Strongbow and Eva* by Daniel Maclise, 1854
FRONTISPIECE: *Thomas Moore* by Martin Shee

Design by Christine Taylor
Production by Wilsted & Taylor Publishing Services
Printed in Hong Kong

1   3   5   7   9   10   8   6   4   2

I should like to dedicate this book to my friend, Conor Farrington, who shared with me his love and knowledge of Moore; to my cousin, Criostoir MacAonghusa, who first introduced me to the riches of Gaelic Ireland; and to my Hungarian-born wife, Ildiko Elizabeth Pokoly Flannery, for having created a "drawing room" environment wherein I have experienced so much of the loveliness evoked in Tom Moore's *Irish Melodies*.

Foreword

Dear Harp of My Country offers a unique perspective on the first artist to have been recognized internationally as Irish, Thomas Moore. In Ireland today, Moore's songs are rarely heard, and his music is viewed by some as anachronistic art—redolent of polite soirées in fine drawing rooms. In the current mood of celebration of all things Celtic, there is the added suspicion that his work was not really *Irish*, and was manufactured to appeal to more "Anglo" ears and foreign sensibilities.

In this book, James Flannery's combined artistic and scholarly approach is infused with a strong challenge to this kind of thinking. In placing Moore and his work in its correct political, social and cultural context, he reveals an artist who was inspired by the ideals of the United Irishmen—a group of men and women, both Catholics and Protestants, who in the 1790s joined hands in common cause. Their vision of an Ireland where the rights, responsibilities and values of all Irish people would be respected is as relevant today as it was two hundred years ago.

James Flannery was the director of the Yeats International Theatre Festival at the Abbey Theatre for five years, and during that time I had the pleasure of working as composer to the Festival under his direction. His passion for Yeats's dramatic writing was the engine that powered the Festival, but this never occluded his belief that theatre must be essentially radical, as challenging to those involved in the process as to its audience. The lasting legacy of the Festival is that the theatre of Yeats is now recognized as of central importance. Indeed, my own work in writing *Riverdance* was profoundly influenced by my artistic collaboration with James Flannery on the plays of Yeats.

This same passion and critical rigour he brings to the work of Thomas Moore, but, as often with James Flannery, he is not content to present just one part of the picture. *Dear Harp of My Country* is accompanied by these excellent recordings of Moore's songs. I have had the pleasure of hearing James Flannery sing on many occasions, most notably at a memorable concert he gave at the residence of the American ambassador to Ireland, Jean Kennedy Smith, in the summer of 1997. Blessed with a beautiful tenor voice and a remarkable feeling for the subtleties of poetic language, he also has the gift of knowing how to reach into what the Irish call *"uaigneas an chroi"*—the secret places of the heart. Now, accompanied by the brilliant Irish harper Janet Harbison, we are given an opportunity to hear Moore interpreted by someone who not only has a deep knowledge of this artist's historical and cultural position, but also reveals a rare instinct for the beauty and power of Moore's writing.

Bill Whelan
Connemara
August 1997

Contents

Part One

Dear Harp
of
My Country

Thomas Moore. School of Thomas Phillips. Reproduced by permission of Seamus Heaney.

Doet, musician, singer, wit, polemicist, journalist, biographer and letter-writer Thomas Moore (1779–1852) was one of the most brilliant figures of the Regency as well as the first internationally noted man of letters identified with Ireland. In his lifetime Moore knew the heights of fame not only in England and his native Ireland, but in America and throughout Europe, where, along with Lord Byron and Sir Walter Scott, he was the embodiment of British Romanticism.

Moore's lasting reputation rests with the ten immensely popular volumes of folk song arrangements published as the *Irish Melodies* between 1808 and 1834. Like Robert Burns of Scotland, he was primarily a lyricist who took traditional airs then just beginning to be collected and provided them with new words in English. In doing so, Moore not only displayed a poetic genius of his own, but, for someone who knew little Irish, was also amazingly faithful to the feeling and texture of the original sources.

Down through the centuries the sense of a distinctive Irish culture had been preserved by the bardic order of poets and harpers that held an honored place in the assemblies of their chieftains. From Amergin—the legendary poet-seer who led the Milesians from Galicia on a voyage quest to a mysterious island in the northern seas—on to modern times, the bard identified his own calling with the spiritual, social, and political destiny of his people. Setting foot on Irish soil for the first time, Amergin is said to have chanted a mystical ode claiming to be at one with the whole environment: wind, sea, bull, hawk, dewdrop, flower, boar, salmon, lake, hill, the point of the warrior's spear and "a god who fashions inspiration in the head." Echoing this shamanistic function, William Butler Yeats (1865–1939) near the end of the last century summoned the power of his poetic ancestors near and distant in singing "to sweeten Ireland's wrong," just as Padraic Pearse (1879–1916), the poet leader of the 1916 Easter Rising, called upon the people of Ireland to reclaim their "ancient glory" through a heroic act of rebellion:

I say to my people that they are holy, that they are august, despite their chains.
That they are greater than those that hold them, and stronger and purer,
That they have but need of courage, and to call on the name of their God.

No one with a feeling for Irish poetry and song could fail to find an echo in Pearse's words of Thomas Moore's famous air, "The Minstrel Boy." Yet Moore, despite his evocation of a "warrior bard" prepared to sacrifice his life rather than betray his principles, is often dismissed as a nominal Irishman whose patriotism ran skin deep, an opportunist whose social ambitions outweighed his convictions, and a drawing room balladeer whose songs reflected merely "a past so deeply buried that it was not recoverable except as sentiment."

These judgments are not only an injustice to Moore; they also reflect attitudes that still limit the development of a more comprehensive and sympathetic understanding of the vast complexities of Irish history. "Nationalism," writes the cultural historian Terry Eagleton, "is a spiritual principle before it is a political programme." Thomas Moore lived and wrote during one of the darkest periods in Irish history—a time when the cultural legacy of Gaelic Ireland was all but dead. Instead of turning his back on the dying vestiges of that culture, Moore sought to revive and redirect its energies outward. Moreover, he did this in the very language and political territory of the oppressor. While earning his bread as an exile in England, Moore drew his spiritual sustenance from the bardic tradition of Ireland, a heritage then just beginning to be rediscovered. In donning—like Yeats a century later—the mantle of his artistic precursors, Moore became the first in a line of latter-day Irish bards whose artistic ideals and reputations have had to contend with the competing claims of cultural and political nationalisms.

The bardic order of ancient Ireland was the linchpin of a system remarkable for its cultural unity. Originally members of a hereditary caste, the bards (or *filidh* in Old Irish),* besides being the repository of the traditional knowledge and wisdom of the Celtic tribes, were also said to possess supernatural powers of divination and prophecy. The education of the bards lasted some thirteen years and included the study of law, religion, legends, mu-

*Today the term bard is applied indiscriminately to poets, songwriters, and even entertainers. In the time about which we are speaking, the early Middle Ages up to the twelfth century, there was a technical distinction of rank between the bard and the *file*. The bard was simply a poet and versifier while the *filidh* additionally were scholars and keepers of the flame of tribal wisdom.

sic, history and genealogy as well as the strict syllabic meters utilized for court poetry. Bards were expected to have an intimate knowledge of the geography of Ireland, but especially the special category of lore called *faoín dúlraidh*, or songs in praise of place. Much of this dealt with the tales attached to holy hills, such as Tara, as well as stories associated with trees, wells, rivers, standing stones and other sacred spots. My own father comes from Clonmacnoise, one of the most venerated of the ancient holy places of Ireland. As a child, he filled my head with stories connected with that haunted landscape of round towers, ruined churches and Celtic high crosses situated on a majestic bend of the River Shannon. As with many Irish abroad, the acute longing of my father for his homeland had its roots in *duchás*, the intimate attachment fostered through stories associated with a particular place. Such was—and is—the richness of the bardic tradition in fostering an extraordinary love of country passed on from generation to generation, even to those far removed from the land of their ancestors.

In many ways, the bardic schools were the nearest thing to a modern university or college. Young men left home and were apprenticed for six months at a time to a master poet or *ollamh*—still the term for professor in the Irish language. But there was a considerable difference between the overtly programmatic education offered today and the fierce intellectual and spiritual discipline forced upon the apprentice scholar-artists of ancient Ireland. For one thing, they spent their days housed in tiny huts that were meagerly furnished with a bed, a table and some chairs. The only light was a guttering candle—and that reserved for special occasions. Contemplation was central to the whole exercise—a carryover, perhaps, of the druidic practice of disciplining the imagination by plunging the acolyte into the darkness of the unconscious through a systematic series of magical rites. Examinations consisted of assigned subjects upon which the students were expected to compose their poems before reciting

The Last Circuit of Pilgrims at Clonmacnoise *by George Petrie, 1838.*

them in public. Again, the actual process of composition was carried out in total darkness, lasting sometimes over a day and night, so as to engage the soul as well as the mind. Yeats recalled this practice in his lifelong pursuit of occult experience as a pathway to combined spiritual and aesthetic enlightenment.

Perhaps the most remarkable aspect of the early bardic tradition is that it was entirely oral. The bards were expected to memorize vast amounts of poetry, stories and historical material which they recited to the accompaniment of a harper in formal ceremonies hosted by the tribal chieftains to whom they vowed allegiance. In effect, the bards functioned as public officials with a high professional status in the eyes of their fellow countrymen. Within the court they also exercised the role of public intellectuals and principal advisors to the chieftains. Hence, besides their cultural influence they also held real political power.

So long as the cultural integrity of Gaelic Ireland held firm, the position of the bardic order was secure. With the Norman Conquest in 1169, however, the great centers of patronage for the bards began to decline. The odes, elegies and satires of the earlier bardic tradition were far too complex in subject matter and form to be set to actual melodies. What the Normans introduced was the Continental tradition of the troubadour or songwriter. Gradually, the performance ensemble of poet and harper collapsed, being replaced by singers who accompanied their own compositions with varying degrees of literary and musical proficiency, or poets who recited unaccompanied poems and stories. Before long the poets and harpers were viewed as mere entertainers rather than revered men of learning.

Still, even under these straitened circumstances the bards retained a vestigial remnant of their former role as custodians of the tribal memory as well as praise-sayers and satirists. Chieftains paid well to have their virtues celebrated while worrying that their faults might be exposed to public ridicule. Bearing in mind that the Gaelic word *flaimheal* means both prince-like and generous, the most venomous satires were directed against those who were niggardly with their offerings. Many of the bards no longer had permanent homes, but their potential curse may have been reason enough for a chieftain to grant them hospitality.

Beginning with the defeat of the great Gaelic chieftain Red Hugh O'Neill at the Battle of Kinsale (1601), seventeenth-century Ireland suffered a series of catastrophic defeats that all but destroyed the native culture. With the loss of their aristocratic patronage, the bardic order fell to pieces. By mid-century, the bardic schools had entirely disappeared and numbers of highly educated men found that there was no longer any support for their once honorable profession. The culminating blow was the departure of the last of the Irish nobility for the Continent—the tragic "Flight of the Wild Geese"—after the Battle of the Boyne (1690) and the ensuing Williamite conquest. The bardic oral tradition became the folklore of the people while the descendants of the bards, reduced to near beggary, wandered the countryside, their collective voice, in the words of John Montague, "a long drawn out death song of an order, monstrous in its intensity, like a dog howling after its master."

The world laid low and the wind blew—like a dust—
Alexander, Caesar, and all their followers.
Tara is proud; and look how it stands with Troy.
And even the English—maybe they might die.

Loss of our learning brought darkness, weakness and woe
On me and mine. Amid these unrighteous hordes
Oafs have entered the place of the poets
And taken the light of the school from everyone.

These lines, ascribed to the Gaelic poet Eoghan Rua O'Suillebháin (1745–1784), are reputed to have been spoken when a priest dispossessed him of his comfortable place by the fire, leaving him to find accommodation "in the turf" at the back of the room. An Irish Robert Burns whose verses were quoted by the peasantry over a century after his death, "Owen of the Sweet Mouth" earned his living as a *spailpín*, or itinerant laborer, and as an occasional hedge schoolmaster. The mingled Latinate and Irish imagery in the poem is typical of the reverence for higher learning still preserved among the people—a tradition magnificently captured in Brian Friel's contemporary play, *Translations*. From the standpoint of the artist, however, what is being described is not just personal humiliation but the destruction of an entire civilization. As the Irish historian Geoffrey Keating (1570–1644) wrote following the Battle of Kinsale: "There were lost beside nobility and honor, generosity and great deeds, hospitality and kindliness, courtesy and noble birth, culture and activity, strength and courage, valor and steadfastness, the authority and sovereignty of the Gaels to the end of time."

Desperate as the situation described by Keating and O'Suillebháin, things would have remained much worse were it not for the efforts of a group of Anglo-Irish gentleman-scholars who, towards the end of the eighteenth century, were determined to answer long-standing English charges that their countrymen were ignorant, rebellious savages who knew nothing of civilization until the laws, language and manners of England had been bestowed upon them. Ironically, this time these charges were being made by a group of *Scottish* intellectuals determined to advance their own claim to an indigenous Celtic culture of distinguished lineage. That claim was based primarily on the publication in the early 1760s of a series of supposed "translations" from a third-century Scottish bard named Ossian. The sources of the Ossianic poems of James Macpherson (1736–1796) were later proven to be fraudulent and, in any case, he was an appalling writer. Nonetheless, the Ossianic poems of Macpherson created a "Celtomania" that in the last decade of the century spread throughout Europe, exerted a major influence on the Romantics and, in the process, created an audience for the far more authoritative art of Thomas Moore.

Nowhere was the frenzy for things Celtic greater than in Germany. There the poems of Macpherson were seized upon by the folklorist and poet Johann Gottfried von Herder (1744–1803), who fused his admiration for Ossian with an enthusiasm for Homer, Shakespeare and a wide interest in folk culture as a source of national identity. For a brief time German scholars confused Celtic with authentic Teutonic material in their search for the *Urmythologie* of Germany's own ancestral *Volk*. That effort ultimately led to the establishment in Germany of university programs in Celtic studies that, over the next century, were to have a key role in vindicating Ireland's claim to a distinctive culture and, with that, political independence.

Patrick O'Neill points out in his definitive study of the relationship between German and Irish literature that, thanks to Ossian, the Gaelic mind made a greater impact on the Continent than it had since the missionary expansion of Irish Christianity in the early Middle Ages. The Ossianic poems had a particularly powerful influence on the imagination of the greatest literary figure of

JAMES MACPHERSON Esq.ʳ

the age: Johann Wolfgang von Goethe (1749–1832). Goethe was so taken with them that, word by word, he painfully pored over the thirty-eight lines of Macpherson's made-up Gaelic "source." In 1779 Goethe published a semi-autobiographical novel, *The Sorrows of Young Werther*, in which the hero identified his own feelings with the world-weary languor of the legendary bard:

> Ossian has superseded Homer in my head. To what a world does the illustrious bard carry me! To wander over pathless wilds, surrounded by impetuous whirlwinds, where by the feeble light of the moon, we see the spirits of our ancestors: to hear from the mountain-tops, mid the roar of torrents, their plaintive sounds issuing from deep caverns, and the mossy tomb of the warrior by whom she was adored. I meet this bard with silver hair: he wanders in the valley, he seeks the footsteps of his fathers, and alas! he finds only their tombs . . .

Astonishing as it may seem, here within these liquid strains of pseudo-Celtic sentiment occur the first soundings of a Romantic note that would echo not only in Germany but throughout Europe for another hundred years. No fewer than twenty-six separate editions of *Werther* appeared in England before 1800. In France its impact was even greater. Napoleon claimed to have read the novel seven times. Moreover, the fitful yearnings of Ossian inspired men with the view that the rights of the individual are of greater consequence than social conventions and that a desire for freedom based on an atavistic sense of national character can provide a more legitimate form of government than one imposed from without. Arguably, "the taste for Ossian" struck the first note of a revolutionary ardor that was to be felt in France, Germany and many other countries, including Ireland.

Ironically, contemporary Irish claims concerning the native origins of "Ossianic" poetry were at first ignored. Macpherson himself argued hotly against any such suggestion. He acknowledged the existence of some similar Irish ballads, but noted with scorn their barbarous tone as against the Homeric-Biblical-Miltonic grandeur of the Scottish Ossian. The fact of the matter, as modern scholars have shown, is that the Scottish Highlands and Ireland shared a common Gaelic literary heritage until at least the beginning of the eighteenth century. The original Ossianic poems are concerned with the legendary *Fianna*, a band of the professional soldiers under the leadership of Finn MacCool, the father of Oisin in pre-Christian Ireland. A century following Macpherson's publication, the Irish forcefully asserted their own claim to an ancient heroic lineage in the form of an armed rebellion led by an elite conspiratorial band of militant nationalists known as the Fenian Brotherhood. That rebellion failed, but it is worth noting that the political party which emerged out of the Easter Rising to lead Ireland throughout most of the current century is *Fianna Fail* ("The Soldiers of Destiny"). As Macauley once remarked, the history of Ireland is like "[a] thin crust of ashes, beneath which lava is still flowing."

Even Tom Moore, whose own Romantic yearnings were always tempered by an Augustan sense of proportion, had a brief fling with the effusive style of Macpherson while an eighteen-year-old student at Trinity College, Dublin. Significantly, his youthful "Extract for a Poem in Imitation of Ossian" contained a note of angry defiance that is utterly missing in the Scottish poet:

> O! children of Erin! you'r robbed; why not rouse from your slumber
> of Death?—Oh! why not assert her lov'd cause, and
> strike off her chains and your own—and hail her to freedom
> and peace! Oh! that Ossian now flourished and here; he would
> tell us the deeds of our fires, and swell up our souls to be
> brave!—for his Harp flow'd a torrent around, and incitement
> enforc'd as the stream!—but silence now reigns o'er the wires.

One reason for the absence of a similar feeling in Macpherson is that the Act of Union binding the Scottish and English parliaments together in 1707 had effectively ended Scotland's status as an independent nation. The Scottish Highlanders, like the Irish, were previously regarded as a rude and barbarous people who needed to be subdued. But now, thanks to the fantasy images created by Macpherson, they were transformed into exemplars of a long-lost primitive splendor that, with the right promotion, could be made as appealing to the English as to the Scots. The public relations aspects of this endeavor were not lost on the Irish, including Moore—but a significant difference is that, unlike Ireland, following the tragic revolutionary adventure and defeat of "Bonnie Prince Charlie" in 1746, Scotland was no longer perceived as a threat. Thoroughly realistic and practical, the nobility and rising middle classes of Scotland thereafter gave their allegiance to the House of Hanover and British mercantile interests. Their reward was that, even as beguiling tourist images of Celtic Scotland spread abroad, the country was turning its central belt, where most of the people lived, into one of the most intensely industrialized areas in the world.

Nothing exhibits the contrast between Scotland and Ireland more vividly than the attitudes held down to the present day towards their respective "National Poets," Robert Burns and Thomas Moore. Burns (1759–1796), who jocularly referred to himself as "His Bardship" or "Bardie," was a well-educated son of a tenant farmer who played the role of a country bumpkin in the fashionable drawing rooms, clubs, university dining rooms and taverns of Edinburgh. The Act of Union had brought with it a crisis of cultural identity for the Scots, but Burns provided for them a connection with their roots by combining folk melodies from a wide variety of sources (including the Highlands, the Border Counties, England and Ireland) with lyrics written in a literary dialect based on Lallans Scots, the historic form of English spoken in his native Ayreshire. Burns knew and admired the work of Macpherson, but the only explicitly Celtic elements in his own work are some of the airs he set, and his boisterously roguish public persona.

It is sometimes difficult, especially for an Irishman, to fathom how this lusty, irreverent, outspoken rebel managed to win the affections of the upstanding Scots of his time—an affair of the heart that continues today in Burns Night suppers celebrated everywhere loyal Scots gather, replete with haggis, toasts to the Queen and reverent recitations of the bard's poetry in pseudo-Scottish accents by tartan-clad, teary-eyed purveyors of Caledonian coziness. And yet something of meaning does come through on these all-male occasions, particularly at the close of the evening when the names of recently departed Burnsians are read and, arms linked, a chorus of "Auld Lang Syne" is sung by the circled assembly. Artificial as the overtly Celtic posturing can sometimes appear, and contrary as the radically anarchic sentiments of Burns are to the actual values of the successful doctors, lawyers and businessmen who normally attend these functions, what is also evident is that the rough outpouring of feeling (there is all the difference between a gutteral "och" and a breathless "o"), the slightly archaic eroticism ("dearie," "canna get," "ilka lassie" and the like) along with the wonderfully evocative natural details ("Thou green-crested lapwing, thy screaming forbear") all come together to express common truths that lie beneath the world of appearances. The earthy qualities of Burns are, in fact, the very key to his lasting appeal.

The same bold and exuberant earthiness is found in the poetry of Gaelic writers like Eoghan Rua O'Suillebháin, but not heard in an Anglo-Irish literary idiom until the plays of John Millington Synge at the turn of this century. In contrast to Burns, however, the plays of Synge were furiously rejected by the audiences at the Abbey Theatre on the grounds that they were immoral and therefore false to the authentic lives of the peasants being portrayed. How, then, to explain the enduring honor given to Burns as the spirit of Scotland personified, while a host of Irish artists from Moore to Yeats, Synge, and Joyce have been greeted with blatant hostility? Part of the answer lies in the fact that Scotland arrived at political and economic stability far earlier than Ireland. But this occurred at the cost of accepting, both symbolically and practically, an anglicized way of life. What Burns provided for respectable, well-educated Scotsmen was a link with the past that enabled them to maintain a semblance of their Celtic heritage. In other words, Burns, the apostle of the common man, created through his poetic genius a new democracy of the spirit that, although rooted in peasant values, was one to which all Scotsmen could aspire.

The situation faced by Moore was a far more complex and challenging one than that of Burns. What Moore undertook was not only to recover the aristocratic Gaelic culture of Ireland, as embodied in the poetry and music of the bardic order, but to find a new audience capable of responding to the refinements of such a highly sophisticated art. His problems were vastly complicated by the tortuous entanglements of eighteenth-century Irish life.

Eighteenth-century Ireland was a desperately and dangerously divided society. Political leadership was firmly in the hands of the Protestant Ascendancy—and they were originally just that, most of them: soldiers of fortune, merchants, carpetbaggers and king's courtiers who, by virtue of royal grants of land and other forms of patronage, had suddenly ascended to power and privilege. Overnight some of them acquired high-sounding titles: Mr. Browne became the Earl of Kenmare and Mr. Smith the Earl of Bantry. For the most part, these newly created Anglo-Irish landed gentry had little interest in any culture, much less that of the Irish peasantry. Oliver Goldsmith (1728–1774) aptly described them as a people "who spend their whole lives running after a hare, drinking to be drunk, and getting every girl who will let them with child."

From the standpoint of the peasantry, the Anglo-Irish were an alien presence towards whom they felt neither affection nor allegiance. In contrast, the twelfth-century Norman invaders had, within a relatively short period of time, become an integral part of the cultural and political landscape of Ireland. Intermarrying with the natives and exchanging their own Norman French for Gaelic, adopting Irish ways, including the poetry and music of the bards, as well as Irish laws, the Normans were, as the saying goes, *Hibernicis ipsis hiberniore* ("more Irish than the Irish"). Perhaps the greatest contrast between the old and the new settlers of Ireland was that, while the Normans confiscated great tracts of territory, and built castles to defend them, they nonetheless left untouched the sacred bond between the native people and the land they inhabited. That bond was originally forged by the druids, the high priests of Celtic nature worship. As we have seen, it was a bond celebrated from the time of Amergin in poems that commingled the identity of God, man, and nature. When Ireland adopted the Christianity of St. Patrick in the fifth century, the unique form of religious belief and practice that emerged was heavily influenced by the older pagan traditions. As Thomas Cahill has written, the Celtic Christianity of early Ireland was founded on "the natural mysticism of the Irish—which already told them the world was holy—all the world, not just parts. It was on this sturdy insight that Patrick choreographed the sacred dance of Irish sacramental life as a sacramentality not limited to the symbolic actions of the church's liturgy but open to the whole created universe."

The ancient understanding of Ireland as an *Insula sacra* ("holy island") goes back to at least the sixth century B.C., where it is mentioned in Greek texts. This concept, which was to provide the foundation of modern Irish nationalism, had a powerful influence on the way in which the Irish conceived the ownership of land. According to tradition, in pre-Christian Ireland the *ollamh* handed the newly elected chieftain a rod symbolizing his union with the goddess of the land. Thus, the holding of land was a fleeting, terminable thing, determined by the rights bestowed upon the chieftain because of his innate personal qualities as a leader rather than by purchase. In other words, an Irish chieftain held authority over territory and people, but did not own them. Moreover, despite the cultural unity mentioned earlier—a unity of common intellectual and spiritual possessions fostered mainly by the bards—the country of Ireland actually consisted of a number of small, autonomous tribal units of territory called *tuatha*, each headed by its own chieftain. The *tuatha* were, in turn, grouped into five larger units known as *coicid*, or provinces. Significantly, the fifth province did not exist in reality; instead it was the imaginative concept of an ideal Erin held in the Gaelic mind.

Despite its seemingly unstable nature and the very Irish tendency of the chieftains to quarrel among themselves (intertribal warfare was often viewed as just another form of sport), this loose governmental system functioned throughout most of Ireland until the early sixteenth century. In theory, the Hiberno-Norman lords owed their allegiance to the Crown, but in practice they behaved with the same local autonomy as the Gaelic chieftains. The only part of Ireland firmly under Royal control was "the Pale," an area consisting of Dublin and a few hundred square miles of the surrounding countryside. The term "beyond the Pale" still refers to an outlandish defiance of civilized behavior—and that is exactly how the Irish were viewed in their continued refusal to bow to English rule. In 1534, Henry VIII determined that this anarchic state of affairs had to end. By royal statute he declared himself "King of Ireland" and pronounced that all Irish lands were to be surrendered to the Crown and then re-granted to his own loyalists. This was the beginning of the end of the old Gaelic way of life.

Strategies of colonization throughout the world have been based upon the destruction of indigenous languages as a way of undermining cultural identity. Under Henry, a systematic campaign was waged to eradicate the native Celtic languages of Wales, Scotland and Ireland. This campaign achieved considerable success in Wales and Scotland, where the upper classes welcomed anglicization as an opportunity to share in the power structure of the nascent Empire. But the attempt to exercise a similar strategy in Ireland met with fierce resistance, thanks in part to the strength of the Gaelic culture but also because the nobility, both Hiberno-Norman and Gaelic, retained their allegiance to the Roman Catholic Church. In response, Henry proscribed not only the Irish language but all outward signs of traditional Irish Catholicism. Under the Tudor government abbeys were wrecked, holy relics burned and Catholic clergymen enjoined to preach only in the English language. As with the European colonization of Africa and the Americas, the native Irish were viewed simply as appendages of the territory to be conquered. Centuries-old beliefs and values were ignored or denigrated with an arrogant contempt. This fundamental lack of respect for a culture based on spiritual rather than material values—a culture that emphasized *being* and not *having*—left a lasting legacy of sullen hatred towards the oppressor.

Elizabeth I carried on the ruthless policies of her father, but with even greater severity. Under her rule, no less than six separate rebellions took place and were repressed with a scorched-earth policy designed to deprive the rebels of food, succor and recruits—and in the process taking a horrific toll on the lives of ordinary civilians. Under James I, who became King in 1603, an ultimately even more devastating weapon of coercion was devised, that of planting settlers as a means of stabilizing English rule. Modestly successful plantations had previously been made in various parts of Ireland, but now an all-out campaign was waged in Ulster, historically the most intensely Gaelic and Catholic province of the whole country. This amounted, in the words of historian Roy Foster, to "tearing Gaelicism out by the roots."

Ironically, many of the new settlers were desperately poor Lowland Scots who had themselves been dispossessed from their own holdings by land clearances designed by the Scottish and English aristocracy to promote large-scale sheep farming. Fiercely Calvinistic, the new settlers of Ulster were forced to exist side-by-side with the former proprietors of the land, who were now in the servile position of laborers. The tensions between them were profoundly psychological as well as political, social, economic and religious. To compound the problem, the planters were themselves beholden to absentee landlords to whom they owed regular rental fees. Therein, at nearly four hundred years remove, are the root causes of the current conflict in Northern Ireland.

The course of events subsequent to the Ulster plantations is an unremitting cycle of repression followed by retaliation followed by retribution. In September 1641 what the Protestants had long been dreading occurred when the Catholics of Ulster struck swiftly and forcefully for the return of their lands. The annual Twelfth of July Orange Day parades in Belfast still commemorate on grotesquely painted banners the massacre of some one hundred men, women and children who were flung from a bridge in Portadown to drown in the chilly waters of the River Bann below. Before the rebellion was finished, several thousand Protestants lost their lives.

Eight years later Oliver Cromwell, now Lord Protector of England, wreaked a bloody revenge that remains alive in Irish folk memory. What had begun as an Ulster phenomenon spread to all parts of the country as Cromwell and his zealots set out to eradicate all traces of Catholicism from Ireland. Priests were hunted down with such energy that the elaborate Catholic church infrastructure developed over centuries was swept aside in a matter of weeks. Catholic landowners east of the Shannon were stripped of their property and banished to the rocky reaches of Clare and Connaught—an event still known as "the curse of Cromwell." Many of the Catholic peasantry remained on the land, but, like their kindred in the North, were forced to serve the new Protestant settlers in a state of almost total humiliation.

Even worse was yet to come. When the restored monarch Charles II replaced the Cromwellian regime in 1660, Irish Catholics hoped that he would restore their status as well. Their hopes were in vain. Charles, fearful lest his precarious position be undermined by alienating the Protestants who had helped him regain the throne, did little to help the Catholics in Ireland. His brother and successor James, after losing the throne to William of Orange in the "Glorious Revolution" of 1688, effectively silenced all Catholic opposition to English rule for another hundred years. This occurred when James entered Ireland in March 1689, hoping to muster support for another restoration from his still loyal Catholic followers. His campaign might well have succeeded but for the famous siege of Derry—wherein some 30,000 Protestants survived near-starvation and were finally rescued by the ships of King William after fifteen weeks of resistance. "No surrender" was the battle cry of the Protestants of Derry—and it has been the watchword of Northern Irish Protestants ever since.

Jacobite military operations ended in 1691 with the "Flight of the Wild Geese," who were allowed to go into exile to fight in the armies of Louis XIV. With their departure, the Catholics had no further means of redress save for the futile hope raised in the *Aisling*, or vision poems, of the wandering bards: that some day the exiled Gaelic nobility would return to vindicate the honor of Ireland.

The terms under which the Jacobites surrendered had stipulated a measure of toleration for Irish Catholics, but those terms were quickly violated by the notorious Penal Laws of 1695. Under this code Irish Catholics could not sit in Parliament or vote in parliamentary elections. Professionally, they were excluded from the bar, the bench, the university and all public bodies. They were forbidden to possess arms or own a horse worth more than five pounds. No Catholic could keep a school or send his children to be educated abroad. The ownership of land was the subject of a whole complex branch of the penal code, as a result of which all the remaining land still owned by Catholics passed into Protestant hands. Division was fostered in Catholic families by laws conferring extraordinary privileges on any member of the family who became a Protestant. For example, the eldest son, by renouncing his Roman Catholic faith and proclaiming publicly his conversion to the Church of Ireland, could deprive his Catholic father of the management and disposal of his property. Catholic bishops and other higher ecclesiastics were banished from the country and were liable to be hanged, drawn and quartered if they returned. While a certain number of registered priests were tolerated, unregistered ones were liable to the same penalties as the hierarchy.

What the Penal Laws did, in the assessment of Conor Cruise O'Brien, a more than cautious student of the history of militant Irish nationalism, "was to perfect and maintain a system of caste domination, with the superior and subordinate castes marked off by religious professions, and with different systems of law applicable to them." The most glaring anomaly, and the factor which made Ireland different from all other European societies, was that most senior officials were of a different ethnic background and a different religion from the population at large. Things had to change; and Thomas Moore, a Catholic educated at Trinity College, Dublin, one of the most important bastions of the Protestant Anglo-Irish Ascendancy, was to play a key role in that slow but inevitable process of change.

The Dublin wherein Tom Moore grew up during the last decades of the eighteenth century was both turbulent and grand. If the Williamite Conquest meant devastation for Catholic Ireland, for the Protestant Ascendancy it offered, for the first time in centuries, a measure of security that enabled them to rebuild a capital city worthy of their own self-esteem. The old town, founded in the ninth century as a permanent base of operation for the Norse invaders, had been a huddle of Tudor timber-framed houses, mediaeval walls, dark narrow alleys and ancient churches, all dominated by the feudal fortress of Dublin Castle. Now the city was laid out in a spacious neo-classical style with wide streets and fine squares. By the end of the century it had acquired a distinct character all its own and was known as the second city of the Empire.

Two hundred fifty of the peerage and another three hundred of the House of Commons, with their families and connections, built town houses in this Ascendancy stronghold. They employed the best architects in Europe to design row after geometrically appointed row of these elegant residences in the style known as Dublin Georgian. Simplicity, purity of line and exquisite craftsmanship marked the style: not only of the subtly varied doorways with their ravishing fanlights, but also the swirling stuccoed ceilings, the shimmering hand-cut crystal and the beautifully proportioned furniture that adorned their public rooms. One wonders how much of the sensibility and taste of Tom Moore may have been formed by the splendor and grace of this still most livable of cities.

Two of the happiest years of my life were spent living at the lower end of Fitzwilliam Street in the heart of Georgian Dublin. In the mornings I would go out to purchase freshly baked bread, glancing up the street to take in the vista of the Dublin Mountains framed in the distance. By the time I returned, the scene had already changed in the softness of the Irish light. It was in that crowded bake-shop I learned one morning that Nelson's Pillar had been blown up the previous night. Rumors were flying that the IRA had done the deed in order to clear the site in front of the General Post Office in preparation for ceremonies commemorating the fiftieth anniversary of the Easter Rising. Nelson was a conspicuous monument of Imperialism, yet many in the crowd were angry at the loss of a familiar landmark. "Ah well," said a little man at the counter dressed in a heavy Ulster coat that reached to his ankles, "at least we'll have the first man in space—even if he arrives in pieces!" Humor has always played a critical role in the balancing act of civilized Dublin discourse.

It was also on Fitzwilliam Street that my wife Ildi and I saw the destruction of the famous Georgian Mile—two magnificent rows of houses facing one another on opposite sides of the street, with their doorways, windows and rooftops all in perfect alignment. Opposite our apartment the government had decided to tear down one block in order to erect offices. At the time few people seemed to care. "It's English architecture anyway," was the general consensus. Over the next few years a good deal of the priceless architectural heritage of Dublin was lost because of the same attitude. Too late, some university students launched a campaign to preserve what was left. Moore, with his inclusive sense of what was right and good in Ireland, would, I'm certain, have fought by their side.

Nelson's Pillar in the painting Sackville (now O'Connell) Street, Dublin *by Michael Angelo Hayes, ca. 1850.*

The crown jewel of Dublin was—and still is—Trinity College. Trinity was founded in 1592 under a charter from Elizabeth I with the aim of providing "education, training and instruction of youths and students in the arts and faculties that they may be the better assisted in the study of the liberal arts and the cultivation of virtue and religion." "Virtue and religion," needless to say, meant Anglicanism. For most of its history, to the Catholics of Ireland Trinity College, Dublin, was a symbol of the Protestant Ascendancy. That is not true today, but it was certainly the case thirty years ago when I was a doctoral candidate there, and it was far more so when Tom Moore entered Trinity in 1795—one of the first Catholics to take advantage of the suspension of the Penal Code in that regard. Behind the fumes and furor of the traffic that careens past Trinity's Front Gate, now one of the busiest intersections in all of Europe, lies a sublime oasis of eighteenth-century calm—one of the great campuses of the world. Until recently the porters wore the short-billed caps of grooms, and one can still imagine the clatter of horses' hooves on the gray cobblestones of Front Square. Tourists line up to view the Book of Kells, a dazzling example of illuminated manuscript design produced by Irish monks some twelve hundred years ago. The Book of Kells is displayed along with "Brien Boru's harp," said to be the oldest in Ireland, in the great barrel-vaulted Long Room of the Library, erected in 1728. Much of the campus—the Examination Hall, the Dining Hall and the Chapel, as well as the main block surrounding Front Square on three sides—was erected during the same period.

Frivolity, scholarship and a certain degree of sanctity have always formed a strange alliance at Trinity. That and social fluidity, for, besides the landed gentry, Trinity opened its doors to the sons of shoemakers, distillers, butchers, surgeons, builders and grocers. The latter was the trade of Moore's father— and he was successful at it. Fellows of the College used to be required to take

Watercolor of Trinity College, Dublin, by James Malton, 1790.

an oath of fealty to the Church of Ireland, and, in most cases, to take Anglican orders. "West British" to the core, at High Table they drank the King's health until 1945. Even in my time there persisted a vague sense that Trinity was a smug little world unto itself; the rest of the island was an appendage, with the Catholic majority viewed as no more than a local annoyance. I often had to remind myself that Trinity had produced other types than the Reverend John Pentland Mahaffy, Professor of Ancient History but best known as Oscar Wilde's mentor in the art of conversation. After Wilde's imprisonment in 1895, Mahaffy refused to sign a petition asking for his early release and referred to him as "the one blot on my tutorship." He also described Catholicism as fit only for the lower orders and dismissed the revival of Gaelic as merely "a Celtic craze." Happily, the patronizing manner of people like Mahaffy is far eclipsed by the literary and intellectual accomplishments of such notable Trinity graduates as William Congreve, George Farquhar, Jonathan Swift, Edmund Burke, Bishop Berkeley, Oliver Goldsmith, Wilde, John Synge and Samuel Beckett.

Characteristic of almost all these writers was an ambivalent attitude towards their own Anglo *and* Irish heritage. Perhaps that was due to their status as outsiders in both societies; in Ireland they were viewed as English while, whether they liked it or not, in England they carried with them the positive as well as negative attributes of their Irish pedigree. Even Beckett was shocked when he first went to London to find himself patronized as "Pat" or "Mike" by the local cabbies. The creative tension produced by the combination of English intellectual detachment with the volatile flair of Irish engagement—what Yeats lauded as a fusion of "passion and precision"—formed the very essence of the Trinity character, and that, in turn, helped Congreve, Farquhar, Goldsmith and Wilde to produce some of the best examples of satirical comedy of manners in the language. Some of the same polish and poise in their brilliant plays is also found

Page from the Book of Kells, ca. 800.

in the poetry and lyrics of Moore, while the effortless eloquence of their wit was evident in his personal charm.

The tension between head and heart that fuels the sharp political and social commentary in many of these writers is also a product of their Anglo-Irish heritage. This aspect of their work was intensified when a specifically Irish situation was involved. Such a localized and hard-hitting perspective found its first and most effective literary spokesman in Jonathan Swift (1667–1745). Although born and educated in Ireland, Swift longed to be part of the glittering literary world of London. This was the pathway to success followed by most of the Anglo-Irish writers named above, as it was by Moore. Nonetheless, when in 1713 Swift was forced by political circumstances to return to Ireland as Dean of St. Patrick's Cathedral, he wrote a series of anonymous tracts under the assumed name of a Dublin draper in which he excoriated English misrule for causing the wretched condition of the Irish people. Outraged by the poverty and injustice he witnessed in the midst of sophisticated luxury, Swift, in "A Modest Proposal" (1723), advocated as a solution to the famine then ravaging the countryside that the people eat their own babies. In response to English trade regulations aimed at destroying the Irish woolen industry, he voiced for the first time a principle that would have far-reaching implications: "All government without the consent of the governed is the very essence of slavery." He thus challenged the right of an English parliament to legislate for Ireland at all.

Thomas Moore also was capable of powerful political satire when the occasion warranted. In 1827, he learned that the House of Commons had once again defeated a bill to enable Catholics to hold parliamentary office while, at the same time, authorizing five million rounds of musket-ball cartridges to be distributed to the various English garrisons stationed throughout Ireland. In response, Moore published the following lines under the title "A Pastoral Ballad by John Bull":

I have found out a gift for my Erin,
    A gift that will surely content her;—
Sweet pledge for a love so endearing!
    Five million of bullets I've sent her.

She ask'd me for freedom and right,
    But ill she her wants understood;
Ball cartridges, morning and night,
    Is a dose that will do her more good . . .

Thus, Erin! my love do I show—
    Thus quiet thee, mate of my bed!
And, as poison and hemp are too slow,
    Do thy business with bullets instead . . .

This early poem foreshadows the mature expressions of patriotic indignation
that form the emotional subtext for such later lyrics as "Come, Rest in This
Bosom" and "Avenging and Bright."

Moore came to his patriotism naturally. As he expressed it in later years,
being a Catholic he was "born with a slave's rope around my neck."
His own "ardor for the national cause" was based on discussions and readings
at the family table. Once, he recalled, he was taken by his father to a dinner held
in honor of the French Revolution. While seated on the knee of the legendary
patriot Napper Tandy, an enthusiastic toast was passed round: "May the
breezes from France fan our Irish Oak into verdure."

The poet's father was from Kerry, one of the most impoverished parts of the country, but nonetheless noted by travelers even in the 1790s for its love of native Irish poetry and its "strange preoccupation with things of the mind." Little is known of John Moore's background, but we can assume that he was at least acquainted with the Irish language—an assumption of considerable import given the Gaelic resonances in the rhythms and internal rhyme schemes of the lyrics for the *Irish Melodies*. We can also assume that he carried with him to Dublin a personal knowledge of the desperate condition of the peasantry in rural Ireland. Living, for the most part, on five or six acres of land, they subsisted on an average wage of five shillings a day. Although crushed under the Penal Laws, they still continued to hold masses in the fields with their outlawed priests—an image of faith and courage captured by Moore in the searing lines of "An Irish Peasant to His Mistress." The ruling class presumed that as time went on the national ideals would fade, the Catholic faith be abandoned, the people lose their pride, submit to their masters and become reconciled to English rule. None of this occurred.

Thomas Moore would have absorbed all of this as his birthright. But it was at Trinity College, Dublin, that he first encountered members of the United Irish Society, a political organization whose ecumenical ideals would have a lasting influence on his life and work. Interestingly, the society did not originate in Dublin, but instead had its begetting in Presbyterian Belfast. Although not yet the booming industrial city it would later become, Belfast by the end of the eighteenth century was already dominated by the descendants of the planters, now risen to the status of prosperous middle-class merchants. No love was lost between these hard-headed businessmen and the Dublin Ascendancy with its superior airs and pretenses to grandeur. Their inherent antipathy towards pomp and overt display was compounded by the fact that, as Dissenters, Presbyterians suffered some of the same restrictions as the papists whom they despised. Indeed, in certain quarters they were viewed as even more dangerous than the Catholics. For this reason Presbyterian worship was not legal in Ireland until 1713, and even then was bitterly opposed by most of the Anglican bishops. Until the latter part of the eighteenth century, Presbyterians were also excluded from Trinity College and therefore looked to Scotland for their higher education. While not formally barred from the Irish House of Commons, they seldom had the wealth or connections necessary for a political career.

All of these conditions contributed to the development of the distinctive character of the Ulster Presbyterian community. Austere and unbending in their piety, they were also cantankerous and suspicious of their non-Presbyterian fellow countrymen. These characteristics came naturally given the isolated position in which they found themselves, not only on the island of Ireland but in relation to the dominant culture of England. Nonetheless, astonishing as it may seem, for a brief period a dream was forged in provincial Belfast of a pluralistic, secular and independent United Ireland that, despite many alterations and setbacks, would remain alive until the present day.

Three factors contributed to this development. The first was the impact of the American Revolution, in which many Scotch-Irish emigrants from Ulster fought with unusual valor and distinction—an accomplishment acknowledged by General Washington himself. Needless to say, the economic and social program that independence from England enabled their American relatives to achieve was of considerable interest at home. But the naturally contentious temperament of Ulstermen was aroused and given a new direction by the French Revolution, with "French principles" freely adopted by those who enjoyed the spectacle of what appeared to be the middle class destroying aristocratic and clerical privilege.

In Dublin, the idea of revolution according to French republican ideals was advanced under the leadership of Wolfe Tone (1763–1798). Tone initially made his appeal to younger members of the Ascendancy, many of them fellow graduates of Trinity College. It was also intended, rather more cautiously, for the benefit of the disadvantaged Catholics of the rural areas who themselves had begun to engage in scattered, hit-and-run attacks against local landlords.

As the century moved to its close, revolutionary ideas also gained credibility and force in reaction to the increasingly restrictive trade policies of the English government following the American Revolution. In Ireland, an articulate campaign was mounted calling for the same access to world trade enjoyed by English merchants. Local vigilante organizations, or "Volunteers" after the American model, were created in Belfast and then Dublin to add teeth to the effort. This led to the granting of what appeared to be considerable autonomy to the Irish Parliament in 1782. Real advances, however, particularly in the area of relief for Catholics, were blocked by a hard core of powerful and politically conservative Ascendancy figures. Moreover, because legislation passed in Ireland was still subject to review by the Privy Council in London, little was done to enable Irish merchants to compete with their English counterparts. Ulster was most affected by this, particularly the burgeoning linen trade. Tensions began to escalate, and with them came increasing cries for total independence from England. Significantly, the motto proposed by William Drennan for the Ulster Volunteers, now the military wing of the Belfast United Irishmen, was taken from Rousseau: "Tout homme doit être soldat pour la défense de sa liberté."

Drennan (1754–1820), the son of a Presbyterian minister, a medical doctor by training, a poet and pamphleteer who described himself as "an aristocratical democrat," would at first glance seem to be an unlikely choice for the leader of a revolutionary organization. But what he sought to galvanize in founding the United Irishmen in October 1791 were all of the political, economic and social energies named above plus something less definable but, in the long run, of far greater consequence. That something was the spirit embodied in the traditional poetry and music of the Gaelic-speaking people. Deprived of a political identity, what had remained alive in the collective imagination of the peasantry was the idea of the island of Ireland as a once unified nation. Now, somewhat incongruously, Drennan, Tone and the mostly Protestant leaders of the United Irishmen began to articulate the idea of a modern Irish nation rooted in shared material and cultural possessions—a nation defined by the wedding of their own ideals with the essence of national yearning that can only be expressed through the symbolic medium of art.

Unique among nations, Ireland has as its symbol a musical instrument, the harp. Ironically, the harp only received this official status in the reign of Henry VIII when, upon declaring himself King of Ireland, he emblazoned it on the Irish coat of arms. Today it appears on Irish coinage as well as government seals, stationery and uniforms. Indeed, Ireland's most famous beverage, Guinness stout, is known throughout the world for its harp logo.

Despite its ancient lineage and its long association with Irish poetry and music, little is known about the development of harping in Ireland. The first notable mention occurs in the travel writings of the twelfth-century Welsh ecclesiastic Giraldus Cambrensis. Although little else in Ireland met with his approval, Giraldus praised the harpers as being far more skilled than the musicians of any nation he had visited:

> It is remarkable that, with such rapid finger work, the musical rhythm is maintained and that, by unfailingly disciplined art, the integrity of the tune is fully

Theobald Wolfe Tone, ca. 1790.

"Brien Boru's harp," fifteenth or sixteenth century.

preserved throughout the ornate rhythms and profusely intricate polyphony. . . . They introduce and leave rhythmic motifs so subtly, they play the tinkling sounds on the thinner strings above the sustained sounds of the thicker strings so freely, they take such secret delight and caress [the strings] so sensuously, that the greatest part of their art seems to lie in veiling it. . . . Thus it happens that those things bring ineffable delight to people of subtle appreciation and sharp discernment.

Giraldus brilliantly captured the magical qualities for which the *claíseach*, or Gaelic wire-strung harp, achieved renown throughout the mediaeval world. Listeners to the recording accompanying this book will gain a fuller understanding of this from the subtly intricate harp arrangements of Janet Harbison—arrangements which, like the interlaced patterns of Celtic illuminated manuscripts, reflect an almost divine order of being. It is no wonder that the harpers were an integral part of the religious ceremonies conducted by the early bardic order.

So potent were the powers still associated with the music of the harpers that in 1537 a British statute prohibited their activities, along with those of the bards, because, by singing the praises of the English gentry now settled in Ireland, they allegedly instilled "a talent of Irish disposition and conversation." These repressive acts may have backfired, however, by instilling in the Irish an even greater resolve to preserve this quintessential aspect of their cultural identity—a lesson not lost on Thomas Moore. Writing of the patriotic theme of the airs contained in the 1808 second edition of the *Irish Melodies*, Moore remarked sardonically that "the charms of song were ennobled with the glories of martyrdom, and the Acts against the minstrels in the reigns of Henry VIII and Elizabeth were as successful, I doubt not, in making my countrymen musicians as the Penal Laws have been in keeping them Catholic."

Ironically, the symbolic significance of the harp gained ever greater currency as the harp tradition as a living art all but disappeared towards the end of the eighteenth century. From 1750 onwards a series of books appeared extolling the romantic image of the bard-harper as emblematic of the lost glories of Celtic civilization. Macpherson's Ossianic maunderings were the most famous and influential of these, but, as we have seen, they were based on fraudulent sources.

Macpherson and his wild inventions were answered by a series of academic salvos from across the Irish Sea. The authors were a group of Anglo-Irish gentleman-scholars who, acting out of good intentions but with little knowledge, were determined to win respect for their adopted country. Unfortunately, their ideas were rooted in inaccurate translations, eccentric historical theories and a total ignorance of the actual lives of the Irish peasantry. In founding the Royal Irish Academy in 1785, however, they provided a much needed legitimacy to the newly emergent field of Irish studies.

Initially, the only Catholic member of the Academy was Charles O'Conor (1710–1791), an impoverished descendant of a noble Irish family. O'Conor was also the only member who knew any Irish, and therefore served as a kind of research assistant to the historians and antiquarians who otherwise would have had no access to the manuscripts they were perusing. Other Catholics were invited to join the Academy in what was at first perceived as a non-sectarian intellectual exercise. But O'Conor, a shrewd tactician, deliberately linked his specifically Catholic concerns with the romantic tastes of the gentry and the progressively radical aspirations of the younger members of the Academy.

O'Conor's influence in the direction of active political engagement may be seen in Joseph Walker Cooper's *Historical Memoirs of the Irish Bards* (1786). In the process of attempting to trace an authentic sense of Irish identity dating all the way back to Amergin, Cooper issued a ringing challenge: "Can that nation be deemed barbarous in which learning shared the next honours to royalty?

Warlike as the Irish were in these days, even arms were less respected among them than letters. Read this, ye polished nations of the earth, and blush."

No doubt, as Seamus Deane observes, the initial attraction of this modest academic movement was that "it brought together on the cultural plane, at a sufficiently removed distance in time, groups which were hopelessly divided from one another in the present." Nonetheless, it was but a short step from high rhetorical flourishes in the name of scholarship to far bolder and more politically based assertions in which a glorious ancient past was contrasted with a degraded present. This was precisely the strategy of the United Irishmen under the leadership of William Drennan. In one of his earliest public pronouncements addressed to his "Fellow-Slaves," Drennan depicted Ireland as a woman in a trance and called upon her children to "add new strings to the Irish Harp. . . . Awake, arise," he cried, "for if you sleep you die."

Mary Helen Thuente has shown in her comprehensive study of the cultural framework for the United Irishmen that literature, music and a revival of the Irish language went hand in hand with their claim for civil and political freedom. This is evident in the insignia of the organization, a harp with the motto, "It Is New Strung and Shall Be Heard." From the very beginning, the United Irishmen sought to educate and influence public opinion by employing the arts as a medium to effect political and social change. In the words of Drennan, the aim was to "strike the soul through the senses" and thus address "the whole Man," "animating his philosophy by the energy of his passions." This goal was realized by publishing, in addition to numerous pamphlets and resolutions, five songbooks, several prose satires and four newspapers located in Belfast, Dublin and Cork. These publications generated for the first time on a mass scale what were to become the stereotypical images of Irish nationalism: bards, harps, shamrocks, green flags, political martyrs and blood sacrifice.

The musical legacy of the United Irishmen was typified by a series of patriotic ballads that in melody, metre, and sentiment were far closer to Scottish traditions than those of the native Irish. One of the most popular of these, "The Exiled Irishman's Lamentation," illustrates the way in which practical concerns were given wider utterance through the use of a simple, homely diction intended to have direct emotional appeal:

> Green were the fields where my forefathers dwelt, O:
>   Erin ma Vorneen! slan leat go brah!*
> Though our farm it was small, yet comforts we felt O,
>   Erin ma Vorneen! slan leat go brah!
> At length came the day when our lease did expire,
> And fain would I live where before liv'd my Sire;
>
> But, ah! well-a-day! I was forced to retire.
>   Erin ma Vorneen! slan leat go brah!

Another ballad, by Henry Joy McCracken, a Presbyterian of Huguenot extraction who was later arrested and executed for the role he played in the 1798 rebellion, demonstrates the concerted effort to bring Scottish and Irish traditions together in a common enterprise:

> Our historians and poets, they always did maintain,
> That the origin of Scottishmen and Irish were the same
>   Shee de wea ma wallagh . . .
> Now to conclude and end my song, may we long live to see,
> The Thistle, and the Shamrock, entwine the olive tree.
>   Shee de wea ma wallagh, ma wallagh, ma wallagh,
>   Shee de wea ma wallagh, ma wallagh, ma wallagh.

*Ireland, my darling! forever adieu!

Engraving of Denis Hempson from Bunting's Ancient Music, *1809.*

While some of the United Irishmen may have rejected the romantic antiquarianism of the Dublin Royal Academy, it is clear that others were deeply interested in the remnants of the bardic tradition as a living source of inspiration. Wolfe Tone, for instance, was an avid musician and collector of traditional Irish songs. He also wrote a stirring anthem, "Ierne United," which was sung at a banquet concluding the most prestigious cultural enterprise organized by the United Irishmen, the famous 1792 Belfast Harp Festival. The lyrics themselves demonstrate the practical usage that could be made by combining antiquarian research with contemporary political feeling:

> When Rome, by dividing, had conquer'd the world,
> And land after land into slavery hurl'd,
> Hibernia escaped, for 'twas Heaven's decree,
> That Ierne United should ever be Free.
>
> Her harp then delighted the nation around.
> By its music entranc'd their own suff'rings were drown'd,
> In Arts and in Learning the foremost was she.
> And Ireland United was Happy and Free.

The Belfast Harp Festival took place July 10–13, 1792—a date deliberately chosen to coincide with celebrations of the fall of the Bastille. Inspired by the annual competition of pipers held in Scotland, three popular harp competitions had been held in Granard, County Longford, in 1781, 1782 and 1783. Well attended by the local gentry, there were no political ramifications to these events except for the normal rivalries among the harpers themselves, who complained about the method of adjudication.

All of the organizers of the Belfast Festival had close ties to the United Irishmen, as is evident from the flier announcing the event which circulated throughout Ireland in December 1791:

> Some inhabitants of Belfast, feeling themselves interested in everything which relates to the honour, as well as the prosperity of their country, propose to open a subscription, which they intend to apply in attempting to revive and perpetuate the ancient Music and Poetry of Ireland. They are solicitous to preserve from oblivion the few fragments which have been permitted to remain, as monuments of the refined taste and genius of their ancestors.
>
> In order to carry this project into execution, it must appear obvious to those acquainted with the situation of this country that it will be necessary to assemble the Harpers, those descendants of our Ancient Bards, who are at present almost exclusively possessed of all that remains of the Music, Poetry and oral traditions of Ireland.
>
> It is proposed that the Harpers should be induced to assemble at Belfast (suppose on the 1st July next) by the distribution of such prizes as may seem adequate to the subscribers, and that a person well versed in the language and antiquities of this nation should attend, with a skillful musician to transcribe and arrange the most beautiful and interesting parts of their knowledge.
>
> An undertaking of this kind will undoubtedly meet the approbation of men of refinement and erudition in every country. And when it is considered how intimately the spirit and character of a people are connected with their national Poetry and Music, it is presumed that the Irish patriot and politician will not deem it an object unworthy his patronage and protection.

Interestingly, given the ancestral connection quoted at the end of the first paragraph, only one of the four organizers of the Festival could claim native Irish blood, all the rest being Presbyterians of Scottish descent. The flier also reflected the popular misconception of the time that the harper possessed the remains of the poetic as well as musical tradition of ancient Ireland. In addition, the appeal to Irish patriots and politicians in the final paragraph is worth noting as an example of the high ideals that motivated the founders of the Festival and, indeed, many supporters of the United Irishmen. The same idealism was to be evoked at the turn of this century in the appeal made to a wide spectrum of political interests by Yeats and Lady Gregory in founding the Irish Literary Theatre, the precursor to the Abbey Theatre.

As Mary Helen Thuente comments,

> The harp festival offered an occasion when the religious, political, and social divisions that so polarized Ireland at the time could be transcended by a shared enthusiasm for Irish art and culture. One cannot imagine a less threatening cultural icon for Irish people of all social and religious backgrounds to rally behind. None of the ancient words had survived so, lacking lyrics, the music transcended sectarian and political rhetoric and conflicts, and offered a paradigm of the "Union" of all Irishmen that was the goal of the United Irishmen.

And yet, as we shall see, the Belfast Harp Festival not only turned out to have an extraordinary political influence through its impact upon the work of Thomas Moore, but, on purely aesthetic grounds, contained seeds of division that have continued to mar the cultural development of Ireland to the present day.

Only ten harpers answered the call to appear at the Festival. Of these, all but one were well into middle age, and six were blind. The eldest, Denis Hempson, was ninety-seven years of age—the single harper who still plucked the metal strings with long crooked fingernails. This traditional method had disappeared because, like everyone else in the Gaelic-speaking countryside, the harpers had become tillers of the soil.

The original announcement indicated that expert transcribers would be present to record both the poetry and music of the harpers. In fact, there was no poetry, but the burden for recording the music fell on the shoulders of a young Belfast organist named Edward Bunting (1773–1843). The manuscripts of Bunting, now preserved in the library of Queen's University, Belfast, demonstrate the daunting challenge with which he was faced. The harpers, like jazz musicians, came out of an oral tradition in which improvisation was an essential skill. Imagine the task of instantly transcribing such music, elaborate embellishments and all. Denis Hempson was particularly difficult because of his reluctance to repeat the same pieces in exactly the same way. As Janet Harbison has noted, it is no wonder that Bunting's scrawled notations look like the scratching of a chicken in sand.

Despite these difficulties, Bunting was inspired by the occasion of the Belfast Harp Festival to make the collection of traditional Irish music his life's work. The first of three collections under his name appeared in 1796. It contained sixty-six harp tunes transcribed for the piano plus a commentary in which Bunting claimed, contrary to his actual experience, that "harpers always played the same tune in the same key, with the same kind of expression, and without a single variation in any single passage, or even in any note."

Bunting's 1796 *General Collection of Ancient Irish Music* began, in its ultimate effect, the revival of traditional Irish music that today enjoys world-wide popularity. But it also marked the beginning of a controversy between the improvisation and flux essential to the oral tradition and the emphasis on fixed notation and consistent performance style characteristic of the written or classical tradition. Tom Moore, whose own work was directly inspired by Bunting and yet departed from Bunting in several key respects, found himself caught in the middle.

Engraving of Edward Bunting by William Brocas, 1811.

Moore's first contact with the Bunting collection occurred in 1797, the year after its publication, while he was a student at Trinity College. It left an indelible impression and he later credited Bunting with having first made him aware of "the beauties of our native music." Eight of the twelve airs in the first 1808 volume of the *Irish Melodies* are from Bunting, and Moore was to provide lyrics for twenty-six other Bunting transcriptions.

The individual who introduced him to the work of Bunting was a young friend of Moore's family, Edward Hudson. Hudson was an accomplished flautist and, with Moore at the piano, together they read through the entire collection. Unknown to Moore, Hudson was a member of the United Irishmen. Moore learned of this when Hudson was arrested in March 1798—shortly before the rebellion of that year—and held in Kilmainham Gaol awaiting his sentence. There Moore visited him and had firsthand experience of that hellish place, now a museum filled with the ghosts of the numerous Irish patriots who were incarcerated or—as with the leaders of the Easter 1916 Rising—executed within its walls.

In order to pass the time while in prison, Hudson made a prophetic drawing on the wall of his cell. This, according to Moore, inspired the lyric for "The Origin of the Harp"—an *aisling* based on a tune collected by Bunting which tells of a shape-changer or fairy woman, who arises from the sea in the form of a Siren and then transforms herself into a harp to win the undying affection of her lover through music. The woman, the harp and the music are all interchangeable symbols of Ireland.

The Origin of the Harp *by Daniel Maclise, 1842.*

Moore's closest friend at Trinity was Robert Emmet, also a member of the United Irishmen. Moore wrote a fulsome tribute to Emmet in his 1831 biography of Lord Edward Fitzgerald, one of the heroes of the rebellion of 1798, which included the following remark: "Were I to number, indeed, the men, among all I have ever known, who appeared to me to combine, in the highest degree, pure moral worth with intellectual pride, I should among the highest of the few, place Robert Emmet." In the Preface to his *Collected Works* (1841) Moore took particular pains to honor Emmet's gifts as an impassioned political orator. Both Emmet and Moore were members of the Historical Society while at Trinity—the first debating club in the British Isles, founded in 1745 by Edmund Burke. Far more than simply a gathering place to test one's forensic skills, "The Hist," as it is called, was where students prepared for public life, and, in the process, had the opportunity to explore controversial topics otherwise not permitted by the authorities. It was during these debates in the 1780s that Wolfe Tone began to develop the radical ideas that led him to become a leader of the United Irishmen. And it was at "The Hist" a decade later that Emmet expounded views that were to lead him to be expelled from Trinity and ultimately to sacrifice his life in the cause of Irish freedom.

Among the subjects that Moore recalled Emmet speaking to was "Whether an Aristocracy or a Democracy is most favourable to the advancement of science and learning." Another, which reflected the impending crisis of conscience faced by many young Irishmen of the time, was "Whether a soldier was bound, on all occasions, to obey the orders of his commanding officer." On the former topic, Emmet eloquently championed the cause of democracy. Moore's exact recollection is telling: ". . . after a brief review of the republics of antiquity, showing how much they had all done for the advancement of science and the arts, [Emmet] proceeded, lastly, to the proud and perilous example then passing before all eyes, the Republic of France." Referring to the

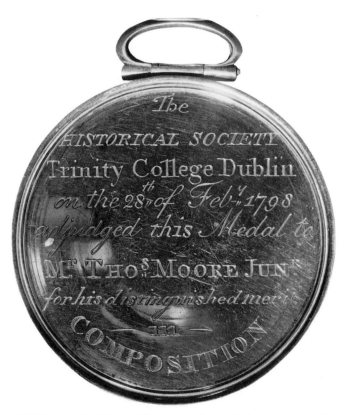

Medal presented to Thomas Moore for his distinguished merit in composition, February 28, 1798, by the Historical Society, Trinity College, Dublin.

image of Caesar crossing the Rubicon while carrying with him both his commentaries and his sword, Emmet went on to proclaim that revolutionary France was guided by a similar love of learning and intellectual freedom: "thus France wades through a sea of storm and blood; but . . . she upholds the glories of science and literature unsullied by the ensanguined tide through which she struggles." Moore is not known for the exactitude of his portraits, yet he again recalled the precise words used by Emmet in another debate: "When a people, advancing rapidly in knowledge and power, perceive at last how far their government is lagging behind them, what then, I ask, is to be done in such a case? What, but to pull the government up to the people."

Moore tells us that on yet another occasion he was seated beside Emmet, playing for him from the Bunting collection when, suddenly, Emmet jumped up and exclaimed, "Oh that I were at the head of twenty thousand men, marching to that air." The tune was that of "Let Erin Remember," one of the most majestic patriotic airs of all the *Irish Melodies*. Moore is mistaken in his source, however; it does not appear in Bunting until 1840—and then as a lively jig. The spirit of the man and the times was what Moore was intent on capturing, and that was also what he wished to express in his art. Hence, in the authentic tradition of the harpers, the freedom with which he occasionally adapted an air to suit his own purposes.

For a brief time Moore was himself caught up in the revolutionary fervor that seized Ireland as the century moved to a close. That led him to what he described as "my first appearance in print as a champion of the popular cause." The vehicle he chose was the Dublin *Press*, a journal set up in the fall of 1797 by a group of United Irishmen (one of them Thomas Addis Emmet, the elder brother of Robert), who were then under government surveillance for their seditious views. In utter secrecy from anyone but Edward Hudson, Moore submitted a long "Letter to the Students of Trinity College Dublin," which appeared anonymously in the December 2 issue of the *Press*. Referring to the professors who had outlawed the United Irish Society at Trinity as "The driveling despots of our monastery" and to his fellow students as the heroes who would bring about the "resurrection of Ireland," Moore called upon the latter to "raise [Ireland] to the rank in the climax of nations from which she is fallen so many, many degrees." He then concluded, "Let us march against the tyrant: let us conquer or die!"

Moore later dismissed this youthful screed for its "dull and turgid prose," adding that the journal itself was "far more distinguished for earnestness of purpose and integrity, than for any great display of literary talent." This is the perspective of age, maturity and distance. There can be no doubt that at the time Moore's letter expressed the genuine patriotic feelings of an eighteen-year-old—feelings heavily influenced by his hero-worship of Hudson and Emmet. Emmet took him aside after learning that he was the author of the piece and warned him that his boldness had risked giving away the position of the rebels. Moore's mother, however, upon learning from Hudson of the personal risk he had taken, made him promise that he would never be so bold again.

Moore took Emmet's rebuke to heart. He recognized that, under the circumstances, action—not talk, nor even writing—was what was needed. His own next decisive action was to refuse to inform on his friends, even at the risk of expulsion, when the College authorities conducted an investigation to determine which undergraduates were members of the United Irishmen. Moore maintained his patriotic principles and, as we shall see, expressed them courageously and forcefully for the rest of his life. From then on, however, he gave voice to his conscience not as a rabble-rousing demagogue but as an artist. Prefiguring the stance of Yeats, Moore drew back from the horrors of revolutionary violence while continuing to venerate the heroism of those willing to die selflessly for ideals that served the welfare of their country.

Watercolor of Robert Emmet (1778–1803) as sketched by John Comerford, according to tradition, during Emmet's trial, ca. 1803.

According to Etienne Balibar in his ground-breaking study, *Race, Nation, Class: Ambiguous Identities*, all nations that emerge from colonization do so in two broad phases. In the first of these an effort is made to eradicate, or "detoxify," the alien influence and thereby restore what is perceived to be lost, broken, corrupted or contaminated. In order to move to a new stage of national self-realization, a myth of continuous, unadulterated and pure identity is usually needed. That myth is tied to idealized histories of the nation aimed at providing an awareness of a "national personality" that arises as "the fulfillment of a 'project' stretching over centuries." Unless that personality is fully accepted and understood by a wide number of people, however, it is not possible to move on to the second phase of decolonization, that of building in practical, political terms a unified nation-state.

The process of gathering the strength necessary for the first phase of decolonization to occur involves tapping into a collective energy that feeds upon anger and resentment. A developing society at this stage is, in the words of Thomas Nairn, "like a man who has to call on all his inherited and (up to this point) largely unconscious powers to confront some inescapable challenge. He summons up such latent energies assuming that, once the challenge is met, they will subside again into a tolerable and settled pattern of personal existence." When it is tapped, however, the great collective energy of nationalism often proves to be an unpredictable and uncontrollable force. Like a bent twig, once released it lashes back with fury, wounding all in its way.

This pattern corresponds to the tragic history of Ireland over the final decades of the eighteenth century. The great surge towards national identity and unity fostered by the United Irishmen also called into being the shadowy forces of racial, sectarian and class hatred. For a brief period, these forces were contained within a cultural and political framework that directed their energies against a common English enemy. But that framework was built upon shaky ground; it quickly crumbled amidst the horrors of 1798.

From the mid-1790s, events in Ireland hurtled towards a crisis. Several prominent United Irishmen were tried and convicted of treason, enabling the government to suppress the Society in 1794. The movement was subsequently reconstructed, but as an oath-bound secret organization. In the North it became dominated by middle-class extremists. Meanwhile, throughout the countryside, rural agitation by Catholic groups known as the Defenders was on the increase. Clashes between these incongruous allies were inevitable, and, when they occurred in 1795, the Orange Order was founded to protect Protestant interests. William Drennan, who supported Catholic Emancipation in principle, was never completely happy about its practical implications. After one agrarian outrage he put to himself the question often raised by his opponents: "Why should we tolerate, why should we commit arms and rights to such savages as these Catholics?" His sister, writing after the collapse of the movement into which they had poured so much of their life's blood, told of her feelings on hearing "a singing procession" of Catholics: "I begin to fear these people and think, like the Jews, they will regain their native land."

In Dublin, similar breakdowns occurred. After the government suppression of 1794, liberal middle-class United Irishmen were replaced by a much tougher and more ruthless underground group of working-class revolutionaries, modeled after the French *sansculottes*. Strangely, their leaders were aristocrats like the glamorous Lord Edward Fitzgerald and the disaffected Anglo-Irish lawyer and revolutionary, Wolfe Tone. Armed rebellion replaced parliamentary reform as the *modus operandi*, especially when, after granting

Catholics the right to vote in 1793, the government continued to waver on the crucial issue of allowing them to sit in Parliament or hold high office. Alternating policies of conciliation and repression caused increasing irritation on all sides. In December 1796, a French fleet, with Wolfe Tone on board, sailed into Bantry Bay—raising hopes and fears throughout the country—but just as quickly sailed away when bad weather prevented an invasion. Crackdowns continued the following year, especially in Belfast. A mostly Protestant yeomanry corps of officers commissioned by the Crown set about "to encite terror, and by that means obtain our end speedily." By 1798 one of these goals had been met, for, as contemporary correspondence indicates, a general mentality of fear was prevalent everywhere.

When the end finally came, it was swift and brutal. The plan of Tone was for a coordinated attack on the various centers of government power, but what actually occurred at the end of May were a series of localized outbreaks, mainly in East Leinster and Wexford, that led to bloodletting and massacre on a savage scale. The campaign in Wexford, the hometown of Moore's mother, was marked by horrific atrocities by both the Catholic rebels, armed mostly with pikes, and the yeomen. In Dublin the campaign was over in a week. The Wexford struggle ended on June 21st, with the famous rout on Vinegar Hill, commemorated ever since in nationalist rhetoric and song. Another modest flare-up occurred in August when a French expedition landed in Mayo, but by the end of the summer the rebellion was over. The death toll on both sides numbered over 30,000; it was the most concentrated episode of violence in Irish history.

Nothing whatsoever was gained by the bloodshed but an inheritance of sectarian animosity and a sense of bitter disillusionment and despair among the native Irish that would only increase with the passage of time. The terrible anguish of the ordinary man was captured in the words of Owen MacCarthy, the fictional poet-hero of Thomas Flanagan's novel, *The Year of the French*: "It was a mad folly. There were men dead and dying all around us at Ballinamuck, with their arms torn off and their bellies ripped open. And in the midst of all my fear I could think only of the folly that had led us there, wandering after that banner onto the red bog of death." The banner, of course, was a large square of green silk with a gilt harp embroidered upon it—the tattered emblem of the United Irishmen.

Two years later, in January 1800, an Act of Union was passed abolishing the Irish Parliament while allowing limited Irish representation at Westminster. Catholic Emancipation had been promised as part of the arrangement, but that was not granted, and then grudgingly, until 1829. The only fruit of almost four decades' effort towards creating an independent nation-state was the further economic and political integration of Ireland into Great Britain. For the remainder of the nineteenth century England's policy towards Ireland was one of forced assimilation, backed by garrisons of armed soldiers stationed strategically throughout the whole island.

For Moore and his fellow patriots these were crushing setbacks. He may have distanced himself from active involvement in the fray, but his heart was filled with pain at the terrible loss of life, of hopes, of dreams, of aspirations and ideals:

> 'Tis gone, and forever, the light we saw breaking,
> Like Heaven's first dawn o'er the sleep of the dead,
> When Man, from the slumber of age awaking,
> Look'd upward and bless'd the pure ray, ere it fled . . .

Oh! never shall earth see a moment so splendid;
Then had one Hymn of Deliverance blended
The tongues of all nations, how sweet had ascended
The first note of Liberty, Erin from thee!

Moore was haunted for the rest of his life by the rising of 1798 and by the wreckage of its aftermath. Years later he stated that it was those events which first nurtured the feelings within him that "found a voice in my country's music." He expressed revulsion over returning to the horrors of the rebellion, yet his *Life and Death of Lord Edward Fitzgerald* (1831) and song after song in the *Irish Melodies*, like the one quoted above, are testimony to the mingled anguish and outrage which he felt while brooding on the meaning of that awful debacle.

More than anything else, the death of his friend Robert Emmet struck home. In 1803, Emmet led another abortive Dublin rebellion and was captured trying to bid farewell to his sweetheart, Sarah Curran. After a token trial, he was condemned to be hanged, drawn and quartered. Before his execution, however, Emmet delivered a speech from the dock whose challenging exhortation inspired Irish revolutionaries for generations to come: "Let no man write my epitaph. When my country shall have taken her place among the nations of the world, then and only then let my epitaph be written."

Five years after Emmet's death, in the first volume of the *Irish Melodies*, Moore honored the memory and ideals of his friend in a beautiful lament, "Oh! Breathe Not His Name." That was the first of two airs inspired by Emmet which, as Moore put it, were "written with a concealed political feeling." The politics to which Moore alludes are clearly those of the United Irishmen. In his biography of Fitzgerald he states, "The government that could drive such a man into such resistance . . . is convicted by the very result alone, without any further inquiry into its history." Again he justified the 1798 rebellion in the following words: "On the right of the oppressed to resist, few in these days would venture to express a doubt, the monstrous stance of passive obedience having long since fallen into dispute." Hence the extraordinarily moving final lines of "When He Who Adores Thee," Moore's commemoration of the death of Fitzgerald, as a blessing for those who would proudly follow in his footsteps.

And yet it is equally clear that Moore shrank from the religious fanaticism that impelled the sectarian atrocities of the rebellion. Intellectually and spiritually Moore was guided by the original ideals of the United Irishmen—ideals grounded in a pluralistic understanding of Irish identity. Although he became one of the foremost spokesmen for the Gaelic tradition of Ireland, he opposed a xenophobic form of nationalism in which only certain orthodoxies were tolerated and others rejected as un-Irish. "I cannot help thinking," he once wryly observed, "that it is possible to love our country very zealously, and to feel deeply interested in her honor and happiness, without believing that Irish was the language spoken in Heaven."

Moore was, in fact, a living example of ecumenism in action. Although a professed Catholic, he married a Protestant, raised his children as Protestants and is buried in a Protestant churchyard. No one fought harder than Moore for Catholic Emancipation. Moreover, his *Travels of an Irish Gentleman in Search of a Religion* (1833), written following the passage of the Emancipation Bill, is an argument on sophisticated theological grounds for his remaining a Catholic even though there were no longer political reasons to do so.

Daniel O'Connell (1775–1847), by creating the first political mass movement of the Irish people, had forced the British Parliament to grant Catholic Emancipation. Yet Moore detested O'Connell's ethnocentric strategy of equating exclusively Catholic interests with the interests of the Irish nation as a whole. This was, in part, because Moore believed that, by "an appeal to the passions of an ignorant and angry multitude," O'Connell had raised "the

Daniel O'Connell painted by J. P. Haverty and W. J. Ward the Younger.

cold-blooded rancour of the bigoted." But perhaps his greatest objection to O'Connell was intellectual. Moore foresaw the dangers of conflating religious dogmatism with an equally dogmatic form of patriotic orthodoxy. "The power connected with creeds is always much more obnoxious than their errors," he commented in a thoughtful *Letter to the Catholics of Dublin* (1810). With the latitudinarian tolerance fostered in him by his Trinity College and United Irishmen background, Moore was capable of seeing both sides of Ireland's vexing religious questions. As he stated for his co-religionists in the *Letter*, "The Protestants fear to entrust their constitution to you as long as you remain under the influence of the Pope; and your reason for continuing under the influence of the Pope is that you fear to entrust your Church to the Protestants."

Yeats was to make the same argument in a famous speech to his fellow Free State Senators in the 1926 Divorce Debate:

> It is perhaps the deepest political passion with this nation that North and South be united into one nation. If it comes that North and South unite, the North will not give up any liberty which she already possesses under her constitution. You will then have to grant to another people what you refuse to grant to those within your own borders. If you show that this country, Southern Ireland, is going to be governed by Catholic ideas and by Catholic ideas alone, you will never get the North. . . . You will drive a wedge into the midst of this nation. . . . You will not get the North if you impose on the minority what the minority considers to be aggressive legislation. . . .

Yeats's words were a stern reminder that the future inheritance of the Irish people was not confined to one section of the community. Almost fifty years later, the same principles were raised again in the 1993 Downing Street Declaration that launched the current peace process in Northern Ireland. As I write, that effort is still floundering in a miasma of sectarian distrust and hatred, broken by outbursts of violence. In this light, it may be worthwhile to speculate on what kind of an Ireland might exist today had the ideas of the United Irishmen been brought to full fruition.

Without question, the most devastating legacy of the rebellion of 1798 was the continued alienation and isolation of Northern Irish Protestants. As Norman Vance has stated, with the break-up of the United Irishmen, Ulster was "edited out of the Irish literary tradition until rediscovered as a context for Seamus Heaney." A central preoccupation of Moore, as for Yeats and now Heaney, has been to explain the Irish People—all the people, North and South, Protestant and Catholic—to one another. Amidst the prevalent threat of violence that has existed during the vastly different times in which they have lived, the humane, compassionate and inclusive vision of these artists remains a source—perhaps the best source—for locating the collective energy necessary to create a truly liberated as well as unified Irish nation.

Upon graduating from Trinity College in 1799, Moore studied law in London, achieved celebrity through the publication of his first book of poems, the mildly salacious *Odes of Anacreon*, and made a year's trip to Bermuda, the West Indies and the United States. While in Washington he had an audience at the White House with the President, Thomas Jefferson, but was unimpressed. Jefferson wore "slippers down at heels" and was ungracious at their meeting. Also, it was rumored that he had a black mistress. Moore, angry at the personal snub and always sensitive to abuse of power by the mighty, avenged himself in lines which lampooned the "weary Statesman" who, "for repose . . . dreams of freedom in his slave's embrace!"

Thomas Moore in His Study at Sloperton Cottage. *English School, nineteenth century.*

Moore was also not impressed with America. In terms that remind one of Alexis de Tocqueville's critique of the nascent American democracy, he commented that "this youthful decay, this crude anticipation of the national period of corruption, represses every hope of the future energy and greatness of America." Snobbery? Not exactly. He also satirized the basic hypocrisy at the core of the American Republic and its professed creed of equality:

> Who can, with patience, for a moment see
> The medley mass of pride and misery,
> Of whips and charters, manacles and rights,
> Of slaving blacks and democratic whites
> And, all the piebald polity that reigns
> In free confusion o'er Columba's plains?

Moore later came to regret these "crude and boyish tirades." But it was nonetheless with a happy heart that he returned to the lively society of London in November 1804. There he remained for the rest of his life, "negotiating," as Augustine Martin so adroitly expressed it, "a complex tradition of exile and cunning which went back to Swift and would go forward as far as Shaw, that of the Irish political man of letters operating in the courts of the conqueror."

Anacreon (1800), a volume of sixty-two lyrics freely translated with copious notes from the sixth-century B.C. Greek poet and singer, was an instant success. Moore was well prepared for his English literary debut. His equivalent of the dark cells wherein the ancient bards of Ireland mastered both scholarship and verse was Marsh's Library—an early eighteenth-century shrine to extinct learning where scholars once were locked into cages filled with precious leather-bound volumes. There, while ostensibly a student at Trinity, Moore spent much of his time dreaming over Greek and Latin folios and polishing the

Engraving of Marsh's Library by Estella Solomon.

dancing anapests which, in their lyrical ardor and grace, anticipate the charms of the *Irish Melodies*.

As Moore's finest biographer, Howard Munford Jones, has said, "Moore's historic mission was to restore music to English verse as the romantics understood verbal music." Overtly luscious as the general tone of *Anacreon* may be, in its warmth, color and hedonistic sensuality, Moore ushered in a Hellenic impulse which exerted a profound influence on Shelley, Keats and Byron. Never again, except in the *Irish Melodies*, was he to equal the sustained inventiveness and fresh-faced buoyancy of wittily seductive lines like these:

> Here recline you, gentle maid,
> Sweet is this embowering shade;
> Sweet the young, the modest trees,
> Ruffled by the kissing breeze,
> Sweet the little founts that weep,
> Lulling soft the mind to sleep;
> Hark! My whispers as they roll,
> Calm persuasion to the soul;
> Tell me, tell me, is not this
> All a stilly scene of bliss?
> Who, my girl, would pass it by?
> Surely neither you nor I.

Translating *Anacreon* also may have taught Moore what, from a performer's standpoint, is one of the keys to his success as a songwriter: the immediate appeal of his opening lines. Who ever got to the point more quickly or gracefully than Moore with "I've a secret to tell thee, but, hush, not here," or "Oh! Arranmore, loved Arranmore, / How oft I dream of thee," or "She is far from the land where her young hero sleeps"? The same directness combined with a subtle evocation of something missing or lost is found throughout *Anacreon*: "I know that Heaven hath sent me here / To run this mortal life's career," "Away, away, ye men of rules / What have I to do with schools" or, introducing a bardic note of reverie:

> I often wish this languid lyre,
> This warbler of my soul's desire,
> Could raise the breath of song sublime,
> To men of fame, in former time.

Besides his natural talent, the greatest boon to Moore's literary career was another extraordinary gift, that of making friends in high places. Moore was not the first artist to take advantage of well-connected friends, but, as an Irishman—particularly an Irishman claiming to be a nationalist—it did not help his reputation, then or now, that many of these new acquaintances were titled Englishmen. Remarkably, the "List of Subscribers" to *Anacreon* opened with "His Royal Highness THE PRINCE OF WALES," to whom the book was dedicated, and, in addition, included the names of two dukes, sixteen earls, nine viscounts and a variety of other nobility!

No wonder, perhaps, that the contemporary Gaelic poet Nuala Ní Dhomhnaill says that the songs of Moore were not allowed in her childhood home because he was considered "a West Brit"; or that Dominic Behan expressed in a popular ballad a view of Moore that still holds in many quarters of Ireland:

> Tom Moore made these waters of fame and renown,
> A lover of anything dressed in a Crown,
> In bandy and brandy old Saxon he'd drown,
> And thrown ne'er a one in the ocean.

Reputations are casually made and dismissed in the land of saints and scholars. But Moore had sound practical reasons for the strategy he adopted to establish a literary career in England. Dublin in 1799 offered no possibilities for any writer, much less one with the strong political views of Moore. The rebellion had been put down, but not forgiven. Habeas corpus was suspended with the Act of Union, giving the government a free hand to threaten or suppress publishers and authors who dared to bring forward seditious ideas. As a young man of modest means and no social background, Moore had no choice but to emigrate. What is astonishing is not only that he won a foothold in a world where birth was normally indispensable to acceptance, but that he did so while openly voicing his convictions about Ireland.

If Ireland after the Union was a political wasteland, conditions for Irishmen in England were even worse. Hordes of uneducated, desperately poor emigrants filled the working-class ghettos of English industrial cities where they were given only the most menial labor. Living in squalor, prone to drinking and fighting among themselves, and notorious for their good-humored contempt of English authority, they were portrayed with the features of gorillas in the pages of the illustrated weeklies. To members of the Tory Party, who controlled Parliament for all but three years between 1783 and 1846, such behavior justified the continued mistreatment of the unruly Irish both at home and across the channel.

Obviously, Moore could not have survived, much less advanced, in his artistic career without the help of enlightened patronage. Distinguishing between the "mob" and "the cultivated few" in matters of taste, Moore chose not to play by the rules of the marketplace. The audience for the kind of art he desired would not be found among the "ignorant and angry multitude," but rather, as he professed (with tongue in cheek) in the preface to the third number of the *Irish Melodies*: "upon the pianofortes of the rich and the educated—of those who can afford to have their national zeal a little stimulated, without exciting much dread of the excesses into which it may hurry them." Moore found such an audience among the aristocratic, liberal-minded supporters of the Whig Party, at whose great houses he was received as an honored guest. Catholic Emancipation was the only broad issue that united the Whigs. Moore became their token Irish patriot. With nerve, judgment and the skill of a born performer, he played upon the latent guilt of his English audiences even as he evoked their sympathy for the Irish cause. Far from being, as his detractors claim, "a poet of bland wish fulfillments," Moore drew upon the historic defeats and suffering of Ireland as a goad to present action. If some at the table were upset by the harshness of the picture being painted, so much the better. As Moore explained it in terms that Machiavelli might have approved, "much more is to be gained by their fears than could ever be expected from their justice."

The key to Moore's success in these extraordinary circumstances was his enormous personal charm. Scarcely five feet tall, with dark curly hair and deep-set eyes, his face had a boyish vivacity of expression which no painter could capture. Added to these physical attributes were wit, gaiety and intelligence— all employed with a natural instinct for judging the subtle moods of his audience. More than anything else, however, for those who came to know him, Moore possessed a refreshing candor and human sympathy. Otherwise he could not have won the respect of some of the most influential men of the time: Sir Walter Scott; Lord John Russell, a future Prime Minister who was to be the editor of Moore's *Journals*; the editor and poet Leigh Hunt; the publisher John Murray; Lord Landsdowne, a devoted champion of Irish causes; and Lord Byron, the most radical of his friends, who described him as "altogether more pleasing than any individual with whom I am acquainted."

Moore indeed became the darling of the English "radical chic," but he always remained his own man. As early as 1804, at the very time when he was struggling to find support, Moore turned down the opportunity to be named "Irish Poet Laureate" because this would involve singing the praises of the House of Hanover. Moore took on a certain amount of journalistic hackwork for the Whigs, but he also attacked their tendency to substitute patronage for principle and to prevaricate where Catholic Emancipation was concerned. When in 1830 his friend and patron Lord Russell sought to discourage him from publishing his biography of Fitzgerald lest it lead to another rebellion, Moore persisted in carrying it out. In what became the most controversial incident of his entire career, Moore was accused of betraying the wishes of Lord Byron—and posterity—by burning the manuscript of Byron's autobiography, which had been entrusted to his care. Recent scholarship shows that Moore fought furiously against his own publisher, John Murray, and a number of influential friends to honor his commitment to Byron. This occurred at considerable financial sacrifice. At length, he only submitted to their wishes because he was persuaded by Byron's half-sister, Augusta Leigh, who pleaded on behalf of Lady Byron out of her fear of indiscretion in the memoir. Chivalry was also part of Moore's courtly code of honor.

So much, then, for Yeats's patronizing dismissal of Moore as "a social ambition incarnate." Regardless of Moore's pleasure in the heady swirl of high society, it must be remembered that he cast his lot with the oppressed, those alien from the supposed glories of the Glorious Revolution, the Declaration of Rights and the British Constitution. Moore's Catholic religion barred him, while the remaining anti-popery laws were in force, from the professions, the Army or the right to hold a seat in Parliament. It was an intolerable humiliation, but as an artist without independent means he had to accept patronage where he could find it. His success is astounding when one considers the patriotic tenor of his songs. All the more remarkable, he remained a man of principle. Time and time again, when patriotism and profit pulled in opposite directions, Moore chose against his own interests.

In a sense, Byron was right when he said, maliciously, that "Tommy loves a lord." But the nobility also loved him. Everyone did. And why not, when he provided so much fun having an Irish laugh at their absurd pretensions?

> The Duke is the lad to frighten a lass,
>   Galloping, dreary duke:
> The Duke is the lad to frighten a lass,
> He's an ogre to meet, and the d—l to pass
>
> With his charger prancing,
> Grim eyes glancing,
> Chin, like a Mufti,
> Grizzled and tufty,
> Galloping, dreary duke.

As Sean O'Casey would say, "You could sing that if you had an air to it." Tommy probably did.

A realist as well as an idealist, Moore recognized that the past was definitely past, the old Gaelic order shattered and the Irish language all but destroyed. Yet he also realized that if Ireland as a nation was to survive, the ancient Gaelic culture had somehow to be reclaimed. At a time when powerful forces were seeking to suppress every vestige of that culture, Moore identified himself with it through the lyrics he created for the *Irish Melodies*. He thereby prepared the way for the miracle whereby Ireland's Gaelic heritage was reborn in another tongue through which its bounty could be—and is today—shared with the whole world.

Moore has often been accused of diluting or falisfying his Gaelic sources. This criticism is based upon a misunderstanding of his intention and actual practice. The art of translation from one language into another is, at best, an inexact one. As evident from translations of Greek drama from the Renaissance to the present day, literary fashion inevitably dictates the form in which a classic work finds a new voice. The better the poet, the more freedom he or she must exercise in trying to capture the feeling of the original text. Good translation is, as William Arrowsmith put it, not the "monstrous gibberish" of literal fidelity, but a genuine creative act which enables the original text to find "another form of living."

Thomas Moore took this necessary artistic freedom a step further, for he was not trying to write lyrics based upon original texts in Gaelic. That effort was to be made later in the century by poets and translators like Samuel Ferguson, James Clarence Mangan and Douglas Hyde. All of these writers knew Irish whereas Moore, it is said, did not. Yet remarkably, Moore anticipates their work by introducing into English certain metrical, rhythmic and tonal patterns taken directly from the Gaelic tradition. What he truly created in his *Irish Melodies* were not folk songs but art songs that, at their best, approach Schubert and Schumann, Fauré and Duparc in their highly sophisticated combination of poetry and music. Moore thereby carried over into English the tradition of the *amhrán moi*, or classical high songs, of the aristocratic bardic tradition of ancient Ireland.

The basis of Moore's approach to the *Irish Melodies* is found in his extraordinary sensitivity to music:

> I only know that in a strong and inborn feeling for music lies the source of whatever talent I may have shown for poetical composition; and that it was the effort to translate into language the emotion and passion which music appeared to me to express that first led to my writing any poetry at all deserving of the name. Dryden has happily described music as 'inarticulate poetry'; and I have always felt, in adapting words to an expressive air, that I was but bestowing upon it the gift of articulation, and thus enabling it to speak to others all that was conveyed, in its wordless eloquence, to me.

In practice, it appears that Moore's method was to let a piece of music work on his feelings until it kindled the fire of inspiration. Sound rather than sense was his first consideration, and in this he was constantly aware, as any poet must be, that mere clarity has little to do with meaning. In other words, it is differences of sound that control meaning because of the direct appeal to the senses. Little is known of Moore's precise method of composition except that he was particularly conscious of the rapid changes of mood that are characteristic of the Irish temperament and are expressed in the tragi-comic plays of Synge, O'Casey, Beckett and Friel. In music, the same fluctuation of feeling is apparent, and Moore was at pains to capture it:

> Even in their liveliest strains we find some melancholy notes intrude—some minor Third or flat Seventh—which throws its shade as it passes. . . . If Burns had been an Irishman (and I would willingly give up all our claims on Ossian for him), his heart would have made it immortal.

The Burns reference is interesting for two reasons. First, it was the success of several volumes of Scottish songs adapted by Burns and published in Edinburgh during the 1790s that persuaded two young Dublin music-sellers, William and James Power, to do the same for Irish music. They approached Moore when he was visiting Dublin in 1806, and he immediately grasped the possibilities of the idea. As he wrote in a letter to John Stevenson, an Irish composer who was commissioned to make piano arrangements of the airs he chose:

> I feel very anxious that a work of this kind should be undertaken. We have too long neglected the only talent for which our English neighbors ever deigned to allow us any credit. Our National Music has never been properly collected; and, while the composers of the Continent have enriched their Operas and Sonatas with melodies borrowed from Ireland—very often without even the acknowledgement—we have left these treasures, to a great degree, unclaimed and fugitive. Thus our airs, like too many of our countrymen, for want of protection at home, passed into the services of foreigners.

Moore's letter, which ignored the contribution of Edward Bunting—an omission that he later corrected—was published as part of the Preface to the first volume of the *Irish Melodies*. So successful was that publication that Moore was offered a contract of £500 a year for a further series. This was a substantial amount of money (a constable could be recruited for a pound a week) and provided Moore, at the age of twenty-seven, with his first regular income.

Burns was equally important to Moore as an artistic example. While, as we have seen, his objectives were entirely different from those of Moore, Burns had taken on the unusual task of writing lyrics to existing music. Moore took note of the fact that, in doing this, Burns had functioned with the "ear and feeling" of a musician. This was evident, said Moore, from "the skill with which he adapts his verse to the structure and character of each different strain." Moore

Robert Burns. Engraving after Naysmith.

went on to add that Burns had an instinct for discovering the "real and innate sentiment which an air was calculated to convey, though previously associated with words expressing a totally different cast of feeling."

Moore was to do exactly the same with the *Irish Melodies*. As Thérèse Tessier points out in an incisive study of Moore's compositional technique, he freely modified the rhythm, notes and structure of a traditional air in order to make it suitable to his own purposes. Thus, for instance, he took "The Groves of Blarney," an eighteenth-century air written in a major key, and completely rewrote the middle section, adding ornamentation and a pentatonic sharpened Fifth. Thus, in a more authentically Irish mode than its source, " 'Tis the Last Rose of Summer" was sent round the world. Yet for this and other "corruptions" he was heavily criticized by many, including the noted Irish composer Charles Villiers Stanford who, in 1894, wrote in a preface for his own "modern" arrangements of the *Melodies* that Moore had supplied "words often beautiful in themselves, but quite out of keeping with the style of the airs."

In effect, what Stanford did was to impose the classical standards of fixed and correct versions of a given piece of music onto an oral tradition in which it was assumed that the performer had the right to add his own interpolations. Moore, in creating new versions of the old airs, both verbally and musically, was actually truer to "the tradition" than his critics. All that is needed in order to realize how deeply creative Moore's instincts really were is to compare his lyrics with what appeared in some of the original publications of the songs. For instance, in Bunting's 1803 collection, the familiar air "The Pretty Girl Milking Her Cow" is translated as a rather banal love song:

> The moon calmly sleeps on the ocean,
> And tinges each white bosom'd sail,
> The barque, scarcely conscious of motion,

Glides slowly before the soft gale:
How vain are the charms they discover
My heart from its sorrows to draw,
While memory carries me over
To cailin beog chruite na mbo!

Moore borrowed the same tune and love theme, but gave it an original twist by exploring in the form of a ballad the betrayal of Breffni O'Rourke by his wife that led to the Norman invasion of Ireland in the twelfth century. Moore's version, it must be admitted, suffers from the forced attempt to conflate English guilt with the sin of adultery. But at the same time it gains strength by confronting the very accessibility and familiarity of the air with a deliberately provocative theme. This is a device that Moore often employed, thereby lending his songs a tension and ambivalence that is not sufficiently appreciated until they are performed.

It may have been for this reason that Moore was reluctant for many years to allow his lyrics to be published without their accompanying music. He explained this as due to the fact that his songs were "composed creations" in which music and words were equally important. In truth, that is so; the greatest virtue of the *Irish Melodies* is their combined musical and poetic appeal. Moreover, other than those of the Elizabethans, few song lyrics in English can stand up to critical scrutiny on their own merit. But that is not the case with Moore. Despite his modest hesitancy about the "blemishes" in his lyrics, it is only by examining them on their own that one can fully understand his marvelous achievement.

The first thing to note is the extraordinary density of the emotional and intellectual resonances that Moore summons with the most limited of means. In part, this is due to the way he combines a mythic substrata with the more urgent and immediate realities of life. Much as certain songs of the American Sixties can evoke a nostalgia with a recognition of still unrealized political and social goals, so Moore's evocation of the names of Malachi, Brien, Bridget, Emmet, Lord Edward, Tara, Emain Macha and the Boyne can, through the power of memory, remind an audience of prophecies fulfilled and tasks still to be completed. Lest one think I am only referring to the effect of Moore on an Irish audience, the bitterness expressed in "When He Who Adores Thee" at the slurs cast upon the life of Lord Edward Fitzgerald by those who had forgotten his ideals can just as easily be applied to the Kennedy brothers and Martin Luther King. Indeed, I have often drawn this parallel in performing the song.

Another attribute of Moore's lyrics is the way in which, gathering force over a performance, they evoke responses at the deepest levels of the psyche. To a considerable extent this is due to the wavering rhythm of enchantment that he employs in lyrics like "They Know Not My Heart," "How Dear to Me," "Silent, Oh Moyle" and "Come O'er the Sea." With their long breath lines and ravishing liquid flow of vowel sounds and consonants blending into one another, this is the language of reverie. As Northrop Frye observes, in poetry of this nature "the qualities of subconscious association take the lead. The poetry becomes hypnotically repetitive, oracular, incantatory and in the original sense of the word, charming." Yeats, with his own mystical desire to transport readers and audiences into the phantasmagorical world of the unconscious and the supernatural, was well aware of this device. Indeed, the Irish poet Austin Clarke, himself a master of the prosody of Gaelic verse, was convinced that Yeats learned it from Moore.

In these and in other ways Moore is remarkably close to the actual techniques employed in Gaelic poetry. These include internal rhyming through alliteration and assonance, with a repetition of the same vowel sounds cunningly arranged so that every stressed syllable becomes part of a larger pattern. Examples of this abound in the *Melodies*. They include the assonantal echo effects of "The Young May Moon"—note the resonances of "young," "love," "glow," "gleam," "rove," "grove," "sweet," "beam," "moon," "Morna." Or the long vowels, diphthongs and alliterative effects that anticipate the languorous, half-veiled mood of the Celtic Twilight in songs like "How Dear to Me" and "Silent, Oh Moyle," with its "Rs" that express an unending roll of water.

Employed by a tin-eared hack these effects degenerate into what Frank O'Connor called "Babu English," like the following example:

> And are you Aurora or the goddess Flora,
> Or Eutherpasia or fair Venus bright?
> Or Helen fair, beyond compare
> Who saw Paris stole from the Grecian's sight?

In the hands of a master like Moore, however, a distinctive note comes into Anglo-Irish verse that has continued down into the present. For this reason it is hard to believe that he had no knowledge of Irish.

As we have observed, Gaelic poetry in the bardic tradition was intended to be sung or chanted. Because of this orality and its influence on Moore, few lyrics in the English language are more singable than those of the *Irish Melodies*. Always the diction of Moore is simple and direct, with few polysyllables to trip up the tongue or confuse the ear on first hearing. Yet within this format he achieved an astonishing range of color by varying, through the use of internal rhyming, the effect of a series of monosyllables, as in the opening lines of "Erin the Tear and the Smile in Thine Eyes." Almost invariably, Moore's choice of metre and rhythm are perfectly suited to his themes. Note, for instance, the insistent measured anger of the pentametric cadences of "The Irish Peasant to

His Mistress" or the subtle lingering anapests and iambs that evoke the hypnotic otherworldly mood of "At the Mid Hour of Night."

The metre of "At the Mid Hour of Night" is actually based on an old Irish musical form called *anbránocht*:

> At the mid hour of night, when stars are weeping, I fly
> To the lone vale we lov'd, when life shone warm in thine eye;

This trisyllabic metre was strengthened by Moore with delicate interlacings of vowel and consonant correspondences, making the English verse pattern stately and flowing with just a faint hesitancy to create a hint of mystery. The tempo is slow, but the moment-to-moment process is always eventful. Many of Yeats's early poems are also written to "traditional airs." He utilized the same metrical pattern of *anbránocht* in "breath poems" like "The Meditations of the Old Fisherman," "The White Birds," and "The Lover Tells of the Red Rose in His Heart." These poems, like the meditative songs of Moore, achieve a disembodied quality through their murmuring rhythms stretched out over several lines.

Another metric device borrowed directly by Moore from Irish music is that of closing a stanza with three monosyllabic beats, as in the following example from "Silent, Oh Moyle":

> When shall heav'n, its sweet bell ringing,
> Call my spirit to the *fields a-bove*.

Yeats used the same technique in several poems—"Statesman's Holiday," "I Cried Tears Down" and "Crazy Jane on the Mountain"—but, most famously, in "The Lake Isle of Innisfree": "I hear it in the *deep heart's core*."

If further proof were needed of Moore's direct connection with the Gaelic tradition and of his enormous influence on subsequent developments in Irish literature and music, all one need do is look at the themes explored in the *Irish Melodies*. In his classic anthology, *Songs of the Irish*, Donald O'Sullivan provides examples of fifteen different categories of subjects employed in songs originally composed in Gaelic. He does emphasize that, while the country remained Irish-speaking, patriotic songs to rouse the blood were relatively rare. Thus, in this regard, Moore was an innovator. However, virtually all of the other categories identified by O'Sullivan are found in Moore. Over forty of the *Melodies* express the raptures of romantic love. Others deal with the beauties of nature, the anger of betrayal, the balm of friendship, the sorrows of parting and of old age, the comfort of memory and the loss of those precious cultural values that encompass all that the heart and imagination hold dear. Always in the best work of Moore, the perspective is deeply personal—that of a lyric poet who, through the power of poetic language wedded to music, makes the solitary human predicament universal. Moore thus celebrates what Yeats called "the little, infinite faltering flame that one calls oneself." In this hard-wrought psychic triumph over circumstances, the songs of Thomas Moore are quintessentially Irish.

Albert Rosen in *The Romantic Generation* states that "in contrast to the great composers of the eighteenth century, the major failing of the Romantics was their inability to vary the pulse; the art of moving back and forth with ease between one strong accent to the bar to two accents and even four seems to have died out with Beethoven." Like Beethoven, Moore straddled the eighteenth and nineteenth centuries and, while it would be ludicrous to compare his technical innovations with those of Beethoven, we can say that, thanks to his Gaelic sources as well as his own poetic genius, the songs of Moore encompass an enormous range of styles. At his worst, Moore is wearisome with his own verbal clichés, but when his imagination catches fire, the sheer inventiveness of his lyrics can be dazzling. That, perhaps, is why classical composers ranging from Mendelssohn, Berlioz, Von Flotow, and Duparc to Benjamin Britten have done their own settings of his songs.

To a considerable extent, the popular appeal of Moore was due to his comic songs of flirtation and drinking as expressed through the various guises of a troubadour, droll punster and sometimes errant rake who, at length, chooses to settle down in marital bliss, as did Moore himself. Again, as in the performance of traditional Irish music in which a slow air is usually followed by a rollicking dance tune, the exquisite lyrical songs of Moore become all the more poignant and moving because of their contrast with the faster pieces. In his playful range of *personae* Moore anticipated the varied comic poses of James Joyce, James Stephens, Brendan Behan, Samuel Beckett and Flann O'Brien. Moore's frank depiction of sexuality contrasts with the Victorian puritanism evident in later nineteenth-century Irish and Irish-American songs with their innocent peasant maidens and valiant suitors whose cloying expressions of devotion are only matched by a paralyzing timidity.

The sheer high spirits exhibited by Moore reflect what many scholars have noted as characteristic of pre-Famine Ireland. Frank O'Connor, in his incisive and engaging survey of the history of Irish literature, *The Backward Look*, cites a journal kept by an American Protestant missionary who in 1847, the worst year of the Famine, trudged the countryside distributing tracts, staying with the peasants in their cabins and surviving, as they did, on whatever morsels of food were available. One Sunday afternoon she arrived at a cottage where, to bid her welcome, the people improvised a dance to the accompaniment of a flute:

The cabin was too small to contain the three score and ten who had assembled and with one simultaneous movement, without speaking, all rushed out, bearing me along, and placed me upon a cart before the door, the player at my right hand. And then a dance began, which, to say nothing of the day, was to me of no ordinary kind. Not a laugh—not a loud word was heard; no affected airs, which the young are prone to assume; but as soberly as though they were in a funeral procession, they danced for an hour, solely for my amusement, and for my welcome. Then each approached, gave me their hand, bade me God speed, leaped over the stile, and in the stillness walked away.

To O'Connor this incident demonstrates the continuance of an aristocratic heritage of courtesy and natural grace even in the midst of horror: "This is a dance of the peasants to welcome the lady of the castle; and we realize that debased, hungry and ragged as they were, the Irish were still a race of artists."

I had a similar response in meeting my mother's family in West Clare for the first time some thirty years ago. When my mother was young the house was filled with music and dancing every night of the week, for my grandfather was a musician. A native Irish speaker, he was also a noted story-teller and local historian. By the time I arrived the little settlement of Clonnanaha ("the vale of the horses") was depopulated; all that were left were the old people. The Irish language by that time was dead. But I will never forget the gaiety in the shining eyes of the people still living in that community as well as their gentle courtesy and their full-throated laughter when my uncle was persuaded to tell one of his Rabelaisian stories. Once an old couple danced for me on the cottage floor to the lilting of an unaccompanied singer. "Mouth music," was what they called it. Like the performers in *Riverdance*, their bodies responded with total, wild abandon to the intricate rhythms of the music. I will also never forget the lament in Irish sung outside my uncle's door on the day of his funeral. At once intricate and deep, the very air trembled with feeling. I can never sing Moore without having these thoughts in mind.

The work of Moore inspired many others to follow him in composing English versions of the traditional Gaelic songs of Ireland. Their belief, like his, was that the Gaelic culture must be transposed into a modern idiom so that its spirit might survive. Some, like George Petrie, Patrick Weston Joyce, Samuel Ferguson and, later, Douglas Hyde, Joseph Campbell, Padraic Colum and others created lyrics in English that have an original beauty and integrity of their own. Lesser talents, however, filled their lyrics with the clichéd Gaelic terms of belittling endearment—*mavourneen, machree, asthore, alannah*—that pass for genuine feeling in stage Irish songs of the period. One does not find these sentimental images in Moore.

Nor does one find in Moore the mawkish sentiment of the songs of exile that, after the Famine, became a standard part of the Irish and Irish-American repertoire. Moore himself lived the life of an exile, but he never trivialized the anguish of the emigrant experience by treating Ireland as a sorrowful mother, her offspring far from home but trapped in a prepubescent dream of an impossibly idyllic childhood. Instead, with an honesty and directness—often from a non-idealized feminine perspective—Moore explored the causes as well as the pains of exile.

Frank O'Connor has said that no people are so divorced from their background as the Irish. He is, of course, referring not only to the loss of the Irish language and Ireland's brutal history of colonization, but also to the wounds of emigration. For countless emigrants from Ireland up to and beyond the Famine, Moore's *Irish Melodies* were their closest imaginative link to their homeland. Rooted in *dinnsheanchas*, a knowledge of the lore of places, the songs of Moore anticipated the powerful feelings for Ireland evoked in the work of exiled Irish writers like Joyce, Sean O'Casey, and even, in occasional lapses,

George Bernard Shaw and Samuel Beckett. His songs also instilled in many emigrants a sense of Ireland as an archetypal source of spiritual wholeness, a sanctuary of values to which they clung even as they faced the enormous practical challenges of making a new life in the United States, England, Australia, or Canada.

As we have seen, from the very beginning of his involvement with the *Irish Melodies*, Moore credited the music of the harpers as his chief inspiration. In particular, he praised the compositions of Turlough O'Carolan (1670–1738), an itinerant poet, composer and harper known as "the last of the bards." Stories of Carolan's genius circulated after his death. One of the most famous, printed in an essay by Oliver Goldsmith in 1760, describes an incident in which Carolan supposedly challenged a noted classical violinist to a test of skill. The violinist, an Italian, performed the fifth concerto of Vivaldi, after which, according to Goldsmith, Carolan immediately repeated the piece without missing a note, even though it was the first time he had heard it. Then, to add the crowning touch, Carolan boasted that he could compose a concerto in the same style, and did so "with such spirit and eloquence that it may compare (for we have it still) with the finest compositions of Italy."

The story is improbable, but it indicates the status of Carolan as well as the ways in which the Gaelic and Anglo-Irish civilization had begun to impinge on one another. Of the sixty-six airs printed in Bunting's first collection, sixteen were by Carolan. Moore set several Carolan airs, but, in general, the melodies of the harper were too instrumental in character to suit words. The real influence that Carolan had on Moore was in matters of style, for Moore admired the fact that he had not allowed foreign influences to corrupt the "native simplicity" of his music. In contrast, Moore complained bitterly of the "irregular structure," "the lawless metre" and the "wild and refractory" harmonies of the airs published by Bunting and the other collectors. He also proclaimed that many of the airs had been corrupted by the "tasteless decorations" of itinerant musicians. What Moore hoped to do was correct these "errors" by helping to "restore the regularity of the form and the chaste simplicity of its character" so that, as in Carolan, "the pure gold of the melody shines through."

Moore was, of course, talking as a poet for whom, in an art form combining words and music, it was paramount that words be the defining element. As Schiller has said, while music has the capacity to create meaning without referring to a world beyond itself, the poet has the advantage of being able to "put a text to each feeling," thereby supporting "the symbol of imaginative power by the content" and giving the music "a specific direction that it otherwise would not possess." The struggle for the supremacy of words versus music in both musical theater and song was to continue throughout the nineteenth century and on into our own with, for the most part, music emerging victorious. In this regard, the *Melodies* of Moore remain a singular example of what can emerge when the voice of the poet guides the creative process rather than the composer.

In another regard, however, Moore's criticism of the harmonic irregularities and elaborate ornamentation of the harpers is all too obviously due to the prejudices of late eighteenth-century musical fashion. Charles Rosen points out that classical music of the period in which Moore's taste was being formed was guided by an effort to bring a new stability to the extravagant virtuosity and showiness of the Baroque style. In harmony, this resulted in an emphasis on the strength and clarity of major and relative minor keys; in performance, on a diminution of ornamentation (which had usually been created by solo instru-

Carolan the Harper *by Francis Bindon.*

mentalists or singers), and a stricter adherence to the notation of the composer's score. Thus, where Handel relied on ornamentation, often allowing performers to bury the melody within it, Mozart incorporated his variations within the melody for the purpose of expressive effect. Moore was all too obviously a child of his age in condemning as "uncivilized" the "savage *ceanans*, cries, etc." improvised by traditional mourners at Irish funerals while, at the same time, he complained about the "puerile mimicry of natural noises which disgraces so often the works of even Handel himself."

Moore had a sophisticated knowledge of music history and theory, but, in this regard, his limitations were those of the time in which he lived. This explains his wrong-headed observation on the relative value of eighteenth-century versus earlier Irish music: "Though much has been said of the antiquity of our music, it is certain that our finest and most popular airs are modern." Popular, perhaps, for many of the airs of which he speaks were actually written for the theater. But lovely as their vocal lines may be, these eighteenth-century airs are vastly inferior in both structural and harmonic invention to the bardic music which preceded them. What Moore could not have known is that the earlier forms of Irish music were composed not in major or minor keys, but in ancient modal forms with a five-note scale that relates Celtic to Japanese and Chinese music. It is partly for this reason that Bunting found it so difficult to record the elaborate harp airs of Denis Hempson. While most western music since the Renaissance has rested on harmonic pillars that impose a rigorous structure on the melody, Irish music written well into the eighteenth century was free of any such formal patterns. As the recordings of contemporary Irish choral ensembles like Anuna demonstrate, the homophonic music of mediaeval Ireland is closely related to the Gregorian modes employed in the church. Like Gregorian chant, ignoring conventional bar lines and metres, the music hovers and expands as freely as a bird in flight. Added to the enchanting qualities of the archaic harmonies employed in this music are the charms of improvisation carried out with enormous technical virtuosity. The very characteristics of traditional Irish music decried by Moore are those that link it to the folk music of Eastern Europe, Asia, Africa, South America and the Middle East.

The musical limitations of Moore were compounded by the arrangements provided for the *Irish Melodies* by John Stevenson. Unfortunately, as Moore himself came to realize, Stevenson destroyed the character of many of the airs, especially the older pieces, with stiff piano accompaniments replete with florid introductory "symphonies" that owe more to a watered-down Haydn than to anything in the Irish tradition. Listening to these hideously incongruous arrangements it is easy to understand why Hazlitt would say that "Moore converts the wild harp of Erin into a musical snuffbox." The arrangements of Stevenson, by which most people first came to know the *Irish Melodies*, did considerable and lasting damage to the reputation of Moore.

Fortunately, as with many successful artists, the practice of Moore did not always conform to his own theory. Forty-one of the hundred twenty-four *Irish Melodies* are based upon pre-eighteenth-century forms. Among these are some of Moore's most effective songs, including "Come Rest in This Bosom," "Remember the Glories of Brien the Brave," "Oh, Ye Dead," "How Dear to Me," "Come O'er the Sea," "Oh! Arranmore" and "As Vanquished Erin."

Declan Kiberd, in *Inventing Ireland*, a brilliant analysis of modern Irish literature and its impact upon the emerging twentieth-century Irish nation, has said that

In theory, two kinds of freedom were available to the Irish: the return to a pre-colonial Gaelic identity, still yearning for expression if long denied, or the reconstruction from first principles all over again. The first discounted much that had happened, for good as well as ill, during the centuries of occupation; the second was even more exacting, since it urged people to ignore other aspects of their past too. The first eventually took the form of nationalism, as sponsored by Michael Collins, Eamon de Valera and the political elites; the second offered liberation, and was largely the invention of writers and artists who attempted in Santayana's phrase, "to make us citizens by participation in the world that we crave."

Far more than has been realized, Moore's ideas and work adhere to the second form of freedom—a freedom that accepts the reality of the past and present as a basis for envisioning a better future. In creating an imaginative rather than a literal idea of that future, the artist differs from the politician (or ideologically based critic) by recognizing that there is not a singular, fixed identity for either an individual or a nation. Instead, what exists is a field of varied forces within which constant negotiations take place. Again to quote Kiberd,

> the attempt to express an authentic set of feelings through a flawed medium runs like a leitmotif throughout Irish renaissance texts. . . . Caught between two worlds, one half-dead and the other still struggling to be born, the Irish writers sometimes had to pour their thoughts and feelings into incongruous containers. Hence the obsession with the encumbrances of costume in so many texts, prompting Yeats for example, to resolve to abandon the coats of mythology and "walk naked."

And hence, one might add, the role of Moore as an outsider in Regency England, donning the mask of a witty courtier in order to better reveal the nakedness of his raw feelings through the performance of his songs.

The performative dimension of Moore's life and work may be the most important yet least recognized aspect of his genius. Like Oscar Wilde, the poignancy of Moore's art is all the more deeply felt when one realizes the context in which he created and then revealed it to the public. Both he and Wilde were famous for their glittering wit. Byron once said that Moore was the only poet whose conversation equaled his writing: "I have known a dull man to live on a *bon mot* of Moore's for a week." Yet unlike Wilde, whose true vulnerability was only made known years after the wreckage of his trial, imprisonment and subsequent death, Moore's public life was a constant dialectic between the roles of convivial dinner guest/entertainer and bardic witness-bearer to the greatness and grief of his native country. It is a mistake to confuse the drawing room audiences for whom Moore performed with the actual sentiments of his songs. Far tougher-minded than most of his critics have suggested, Moore displayed considerable courage in providing after-dinner entertainments that, to a considerable extent, consisted of battle songs with fierce cries of provocation, revolt and potential retribution.

Like all successful entertainers, Moore had the gifts of intimacy, sincerity and, in the fullest sense of the word, personality. In performance, he accompanied himself; this enabled him to sing with a free-flowing style in which rhythm and measure lost their constraints. As one listener recalled:

> He makes no attempt at music. It is a kind of admirable recitative, in which every shade of thought is syllabled and dwelt upon, and the sentiment of the very song goes through your blood, warming you to the very eyelids and starting your tears, if you have soul or sense in you.

Another remarked upon his uncanny ability to cast a spell through the personal conviction with which he sang:

> The combination of music, and of poetic sentiment emanating from one mind, and glowing in the very countenance and speaking in the very voice which that

Fourteenth-century harper woodcut from Bunting's Ancient Music.

same mind illuminates and directs, produces an effect upon the eye, the taste, the feeling, the whole man in short, such as no mere professional excellence can at all aspire to equal. His head is cast backward and his eyes upward, with the true inspiration of an ancient bard.

Often Moore himself was moved to tears by his songs, as were his hearers. Servants lined up behind closed doors to hear him, women swooned, wrote him notes in verse and begged for locks of his hair. Walter Scott, for whom Moore was the finest singer he had ever heard, noted the sheer animation of his features in performance. Leigh Hunt described his voice as "a flute softened to mere breathing." Still others noted, somewhat mischievously, that even mature matrons were warmed with a new fire. "Oh Moore! Oh Moore! This is not for the good of my soul!" one such dowager was heard to murmur to herself.

Clearly, Moore had the capacity of beguiling and transporting his audiences, but he also had the greater capacity of provoking thought. Otherwise, in an age when performers were idolized but not accepted in polite society, he would not have been honored and revered. "No one writes songs like Moore," said Byron. "Sentiment and imagination are joined to the most harmonious versification, and I know of no greater treat than to hear him sing his own compositions: the powerful expression he gives to them and the pathos of the tunes of his voice, tend to produce an effect on my feelings that no other songs, or singer, ever could." Not surprisingly, Byron's favorites among the songs of Moore were those that combined a romantic ardor with the sting of revolutionary fervor. These he asked for again and again.

The continued satisfaction that Moore's *Melodies* give in performance is due, to a considerable extent, I believe, to the fact that the poet was himself a singer. In shaping, for instance, the lyric of "'Tis the Last Rose of Summer," he achieved an extraordinarily moving effect by connecting the images of loneliness and death to the dying fall of the melodic line. "Believe Me, If All Those Endearing Young Charms" creates a mood of delicate restraint and tenderness through the string of shaded "e" vowels which gradually open up on the "a" of the word "charms," the highest note of the phrase. *Spiniato*, a free, evenly sustained vocal line, is one of the characteristics of *bel canto* singing of the eighteenth and early nineteenth centuries. Moore understood the ways in which that technique can be employed to great emotional effect, as in the soft caress of "Where summer's wave unmurmuring dies," in "I've a Secret to Tell Thee" or, in "They Know Not My Heart," the arching melodic line that gathers momentum phrase by phrase until it reaches a climax on

> As the sky we look up to, though glorious and fair
> Is look'd up to the more, because heaven lies there.

Here the floating *mezzo voce* on the word "to" in the final line is only possible because it is the purest of vowel sounds, thus allowing what the Italians call *un fil de voce*, the thread of the voice, to speak. Moore must have created that effect knowing that it was one he could easily deploy himself.

Moore is often said to be the forerunner of the tradition of English balladry with which genteel Victorians whiled away their Sunday evening "at homes." The music performed on these occasions was an amateurish attempt at renderings of European art music; little intellectual or musical accomplishment was required. Instead, reflecting the ideals of middle-class propriety, the songs were, in the words of Kenneth Young, expected to be "lightly sentimental, lightly religious and lightly gay. Essentially they were nostalgic, not dramatic; they were intended to raise a slight sigh after the port and cigars, not a *crise des nerfs*."

Nothing could be further from the dramatic mood created by an after-dinner entertainment of Moore. By linking the spiritual and national identity of Ireland, Moore was making a profound—and profoundly disturbing—political statement. As he once declared in a speech following a dinner in honor of the future Whig Prime Minister, Lord John Russell:

> I verily believe that being born a slave has but given me a keener sense and relish of the inestimable blessings of freedom, and a more enlarged sympathy with all those—whatever be their race or creed and whether they be blacks or whites—who, with even a glimmering sense of what they seek, are contending for those just rights and privileges of civilized man, without which civilization itself, in its truest sense, cannot exist.

Moore's speech was given in 1835, and expresses his continued fealty to the liberal ideals of his youth. Unfortunately, events were proceeding in such a way that the very civility in style and manner of an artist like Moore were enough to condemn his as *passé*.

John Kennedy once said that "you wouldn't be Irish if you didn't know they'd take it away." Tom Moore gave perfect expression to that quintessentially Irish feeling in the soft strains of sadness and melancholy that cast a shadow on even the most mirthful of his airs. Some of these qualities derive from the modal scales of Irish music. But they also spring from Moore's own experience of sorrow. Old age was not kind to him. An exile in England, he suffered the loss of each of his five children and also the sting of enmity from his fellow countrymen who, having once idolized him, now condemned him as an adopted Irishman whose patriotism was only skin deep.

The initial attacks on Moore came from a political movement that, like the United Irishmen, sought to galvanize the energies of cultural nationalism towards the objective of winning Ireland's political freedom. The Young Ireland movement of the 1840s was originally a splinter of Daniel O'Connell's massive effort to repeal the Act of Union. However, unlike O'Connell, who gathered much of his support from the Catholic middle class, the Young Irelanders aimed at a much broader constituency, as evident from the first edition of *The Nation*, the journal of the movement, which appeared in October 1842 with the following epigraph, "To create and to foster public opinion in Ireland—and to make it racy of the Soil." *The Nation* was an immediate success, with an estimated readership of 250,000. Along with articles that taught "noble lessons" about pre-Norman Gaelic Ireland, the Young Irelanders sought to foster support for their goals through the creation of a new school of "national ballads." By deliberate policy the tradition of Moore was rejected as "the wail of a lost cause"; in its stead *The Nation* set out to express the hopes of a "triumphant future" in a "cataract of coloured words."

Thomas Davis (1814–1845), the principal leader of the movement, provided an assessment of Moore in an essay which marked the publication of a series of Young Ireland songbooks in 1844. This essay, while praising Moore as a literary model, nonetheless included some important reservations that were to define attitudes towards his work for generations to come:

> It may be said that Moore is lyrist enough for Ireland. We might show that though he is perfect in his expression of the softer feelings, and unrivalled even by Burns in many of his gay songs, yet that he is often deficient in vehemence, does not speak of the stronger passions, spoils some of his finest songs by pretty images, is too refined and subtle in his dialect, and too negligent of narrative; but to prove these assertions would take too great a space, and perhaps lead some one to think we wished to run down Moore. He is immeasurably our greatest

Title-page detail from The Spirit of the Nation, *an anthology published by* The Nation, *1843.*

poet, and the greatest lyrist, except Burns, that ever lived; but he has not given songs to the middle and poor classes in Ireland.

The last line of Davis's essay reveals the underlying strategy at work, namely to condemn Moore as an elitist whose art was far above the heads of ordinary people. What this viewpoint failed to acknowledge was that the songs of Moore, in their very refinement and sophistication, were truer to the aristocratic bardic sources of Irish culture than the polemical kind of folk ballads desired by Young Ireland. Ironically, with their didactic themes and banalities of expression, the ballads published by *The Nation* owed far more to English and Scottish sources than to Irish. Yet the wide popular appeal of that work was exactly what was needed in order to once again fan the flames of revolution.

Politically, the repeal movement advocated by the Young Irelanders collapsed with the deaths in 1845 and 1847, respectively, of Thomas Davis and Daniel O'Connell. Their deaths coincided with the onslaught of the Great Famine, which, before it had run its course, reduced the Irish population by half, either through starvation or emigration. Davis and O'Connell believed in constitutional reform, but their place was taken by a new generation of "physical force men." One of the legacies of the Young Ireland movement was the brand of militant nationalism that led to an unsuccessful insurrection in 1848, the previously mentioned Fenian Rebellion of 1868, and the Easter Rising of 1916.

Another legacy of the movement was a concept of the Irish peasantry that endowed them with every possible virtue that could be used to contrast Ireland with the pagan, hedonistic, materialistic decadence of the English oppressor. This may be seen in the following stanzas from a jingoistic ballad composed by Davis:

Let Britain boast her British hosts.
About them all right little care we.
Nor British seas nor British coasts
Can match the Man of Tipperary.

You meet him in his cabin rude,
Or dancing with his dark-hair'd Mary,
You'd swear they knew no other mood
But mirth and love in Tipperary!

The idea behind this paean to sylvan bliss amidst poverty was not entirely unworthy. Citing continental models, Davis advocated an economic reform that
would put an end to feudalism in Ireland by enabling the peasantry to purchase
their own land. Over the next few decades this plan was gradually enacted, so
that by the beginning of the twentieth century Ireland was largely a country
of small farm holdings. From a cultural standpoint, however, the ideology of
Young Ireland fostered an impossibly unrealistic concept of the peasantry. In
essence, the peasantry, particularly in the Gaelic-speaking West of Ireland,
now came to represent the character of the nation as a whole. We have seen that
this idea was originally developed as part of German Romanticism, with the belief that in the life of the folk was to be found the essence of national identity.
In Ireland, this belief was linked to an extremely powerful and puritanical form
of Catholicism which developed after the Famine and, in turn, provided a moral
justification for the use of violence to repel the evil invader.

One might have thought that the Gaelic League, which was founded in 1893
in order to promote the revival of the Irish language, could have helped to provide a more realistic awareness of peasant life. But despite regular pilgrimages
to the Western Gaeltacht to provide direct contact with native Irish-speakers,
this did not occur. From its very beginnings, the Gaelic League contributed to

the cult of the "holy peasant" by clothing its activities in a code of moral rectitude that closely followed the ideology of Young Ireland. Thus Gaelic League arguments were put forth claiming everything from a lower rate of criminality to a complete absence of sexual impropriety among the Irish-speaking peasants.

William Butler Yeats, in founding the Irish literary and dramatic movement at the turn of this century, sought to base it on the imaginative—as distinct from actual—life of the peasantry, as preserved in their folklore, mythology and music. He also hoped to free the movement from "the schoolboy thoughts of Young Ireland" that had plagued Irish intellectual life for half a century. These plans were dashed with the protests that erupted over the plays of Synge at the Abbey Theatre. Christy Mahon, the hero of *The Playboy of the Western World*, was based upon Synge's firsthand experience of life in the Gaeltacht. But, by creating a character who was treated by the "fair colleen" of Mayo as the equivalent of a pulp fiction fantasy figure simply because he claimed to have killed his "Da," Synge confronted the very myth of the "holy peasant" upon which much of the nationalist ideology was based.

Yeats, like Moore before him, was attacked as an elitist for defending the right of Synge's play to be heard. Freedom for Yeats, as for Moore, was concomitant with the possibility of individual choice. Maud Gonne, the beautiful revolutionary leader with whom Yeats was in love, disagreed. She rejected the plays of Synge on the grounds that "a fiercer wilder way to freedom" might be deflected "if the crowd began worrying over subtleties that would bring an end to action." One result of Yeats's defense of Synge is that his own formalistically

William Butler Yeats painted by his father, John Butler Yeats, 1900.

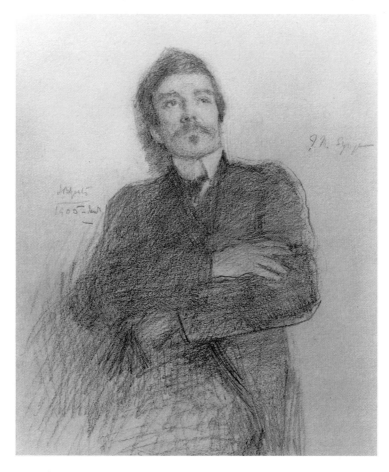

John Millington Synge sketched by John Butler Yeats, 1905.

innovative and intellectually provocative plays were rejected because, in part, they were seen as irrelevant to Irish life. Or rather, like the work of Moore, they did not conform to what extremist politicians had decided that Irish life ought to be. As Frank O'Connor has said, Yeats's effort was crippled from the outset for "the lack of a literate audience." Yeats put it more bluntly: "This ill-breeding of the mind is a far worse thing than the mere bad manners that spit on the floor."

Moore, too, suffered from the diffuse, deeply fractured consciousness of a nation that was trying to define its own identity while at the same time cast off the bonds of colonial oppression. To tough-minded patriots on the move, the art songs of Moore, with their classical restraint and symbolic elegance, seemed, in the phrase of Seamus Heaney, "too light, too conciliatory, too *co-lonisé*." Still others dismissed Moore, along with the music of the harpers, as "ersatz Irish music intended for an elite coterie." These blinkered misjudgments have continued to plague the reputation of Moore. Even today, the editor of the *Field Day Anthology*, a three-volume edition of 1,500 years of Irish literature gathered with the intention of "repossessing some of the standard 'English' names—Swift or Sterne, Burke or Wilde" for Ireland, finds it necessary to relegate Moore to a "middle-class musical world." Seamus Deane argues that the "polish and finish" of the *Irish Melodies* reflects nothing more than an attempt to "'civilize' the Gaelic tradition by making it acceptable to the dominant taste of the reading public of England." In other words, Deane equates the stylistic elegance of Moore with the sycophancy of the forelock-tipping Irish peasantry in the face of their colonial masters. Critic Terence Browne goes Deane one better by claiming that the appeal of Moore's songs to his drawing-room audiences—whether Irish or English—was based on their evocation of a personal sorrow that was then manipulated towards an identification with the sorrows of Ireland. According to Browne, "The *Melodies* treat of Irish history as if its true significance was to provide a drawing room audience with metaphors of its own indulgent source of personal mutability. . . . Sorrow for Ireland is indistinguishable from sorrow for oneself, so send round the bowl and be happy awhile." It is strange that the aspects of art that provide pleasure to cultivated audiences seem to give critics a pain in the head. One wonders whether the soulful songs of Schumann are equally delinquent because they may evoke a passing sympathy for the corruption of German high culture under the Nazis.

There is something inherently tragic about critical judgments that, for misguided aesthetics or political reasons, deprive a people of important links with their own past. That is what has occurred with Moore. For a considerable time it also occurred with Yeats. Cultural discontinuities are among the enduring scars of colonization. Another is a tendency to reject the best in one's tradition, like an abused child who has learned to trust no one and, in a defensive, shamefaced anger, lashes out against friends and foes alike.

Given the circumstances in which he functioned—including the need to support his wife and five children on the limited income of a writer alone—the accomplishments of Moore are remarkable. He was indeed a poet who, by a process of transference, was able to make his audiences identify with their own hidden feelings through the archetypal images contained within his songs. But beyond purely personal identification, he was also able to bring their sympathy to bear upon larger public issues. In this regard Moore was the first in a long line of poet-performers who combined personal expression with a zeal for political and social reform.

To our great-grandparents the *Irish Melodies* of Thomas Moore were as familiar as the songs of John Lennon, Bob Dylan or Bruce Springsteen today. During the nineteenth century a million and a half copies of the sheet music for " 'Tis the Last Rose of Summer" were sold in the United States alone, making it one of the most popular songs ever written. On his deathbed Thomas Jefferson quoted from "It Is Not the Tear at This Moment Shed" in a farewell letter to his daughter. Moore not only belongs to the great line of traditional Irish music; indeed, it was he who made it known throughout the world. In the process, he created a sympathetic hearing for the Irish claim to independence in England and abroad. Moore's *Irish Melodies* were translated into every tongue of Europe, including Hungarian, Polish and Russian, where their expressions of passionate yearning for freedom stirred hearts with similar feelings. What is perhaps most remarkable about this is that Moore achieved enormous celebrity without sacrificing his artistic integrity—an accomplishment of particular note when one thinks of the increasing polarity between high and popular entertainment in our own culture.

Once I had an opportunity to experience for myself the power of the songs of Moore to stir people at those levels of the psyche where art can sometimes attain profound political and spiritual meaning. The occasion was a multicultural conference of white, African-American, Asian and Hispanic men held in Los Angeles. The goal of the conference was to break down ethnic and racial hostility in order to reach a more humane basis of trust and engagement. This involved participation in a variety of activities: music, dance, mask-making, poetry-reading, stories, lectures and discussions. After several days of this, however, things still weren't working; the tensions among us remained as high as when we first arrived.

One evening violence almost broke out when a huge black man attacked the group for making a travesty of the sacred icons of his culture in the rituals we were developing. Two hours of intense debate left us only with a general feeling that the conference had failed. We went to bed frustrated and angry. Next morning, one of the leaders, the great Jungian scholar James Hillman, put things into perspective:

> You know the bumper sticker, "I *heart* New York?" That's how most people go around all day—distant, uninvolved. That's ok. You can't get involved with everyone you meet. But if that's all you've got in your life, you're in trouble, guys.

Then Hillman moved the stakes a bit higher.

> You also know the bumper sticker, "SHIT Happens." Well, that's what happened last night. It had to happen. And it will happen again, if we're to move onto the next level. I call that the soul state. . . . You know how I imagine that? It's when you look into the eyes of another guy and see, behind the mask, the soul, the *anima*, the little girl inside.

One hundred and fifty brawny, hairy-chested men shifted uncomfortably in their seats, deliberately avoiding one another's eyes.

The conference closed on Friday evening with a dinner, some ritual dancing and—at midnight—an entertainment. All week long the men of color were far more open than the whites in celebrating their various cultures. A few Irish guys, learning that I was a singer, begged me to perform something, but I felt that it was still inappropriate for a display of "white power." And then, deep in the morning hours, with the masks we had made lining the walls and the light from the fireplace flickering across the shadowed faces of all the men—now a community of friends who would be parting the next day—I knew that finally the right time had come. Moving to the center of the room, I first spoke a poem of Yeats, "The Cloths of Heaven," dedicating its fragile unspoken dreams to the masks—our secret selves.

And then I sang "They Know Not My Heart" of Moore.

After I finished, there was a long silence. Friends came up to thank me, but I'll never forget what one person said—a brilliant West African drummer: "Man, I never thought any white man had that much soul."

Thomas Moore carried on the mission of the ancient bardic order, for he plumbed the depths of Ireland's rich cultural heritage, reshaping the history, literature, mythology and music that he uncovered into new artistic forms suitable to the age in which he lived. In doing so, Moore prepared the way for the Irish literary and dramatic movement a century later. There were, in fact, two Celtic revivals in Ireland rather than one; and both—in the persons of Moore and Yeats—were led by visionary poets. The imaginative construct of Ireland that they formulated in their writings, in their public pronouncements and by their personal example enabled a positive sense of Irish identity to survive the setbacks and desolation of the nineteenth century and the cataclysmic political and social upheavals of the twentieth. Indeed, without their effort it is doubtful whether the current explosion of interest in Irish music, poetry, literature and film would have been possible.

No doubt, Moore appropriated certain poetic conventions ("chains" of oppression, "tears" of suffering, the "shadow" of death, the "sword" of valor, the "smile" of freedom and the "harp" representing Ireland's ancient culture) that by the time of Yeats had become platitudes quoted with equally vapid fervor by would-be patriots and poets. That is one of the reasons why Moore was so often parodied in the work of Shaw, Joyce and O'Casey—though we should note that Joyce, a fine tenor, loved the songs of Moore and performed them with tenderness and care.

It was, I believe, because of the overt sentimentality with which Moore was quoted and sung by those for whom he had no respect that Yeats tended to disparage Moore's art and example. Yet, as we have seen, Moore could in many ways be described as Yeats's closest artistic and intellectual precursor. Obviously he lacked the brooding tragic passion of Yeats. But Moore possessed something that eluded the far greater poet, namely the popular touch. What this did was enable Moore to provide Irishmen of all classes and creeds with a fuller awareness of their cultural heritage and the value of their struggle for liberty. His songs were rightly described as the secular hymn-book of Irish nationalism. With the inclusiveness of his principles, the courage of his spirit, and the generosity of his passionate heart, Moore was one of those rare artists who has helped to define the character of a nation. As that tough-minded patriot Eamon de Valera—leader of the Easter Rising, Prime Minister and then President of Ireland—once said: "Moore's songs kept the love of country and the lamp of hope burning in Irish hearts in Ireland and in many lands beyond the sea."

Thomas Moore, like the minstrel whom he so often invoked as a symbol of liberty, was himself one who sang for the pure and free of all times everywhere.

Part Two

Moore's Melodies

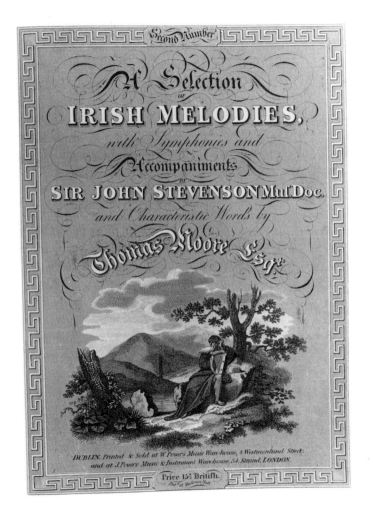

Second Number

A Selection
OF
IRISH MELODIES,

with Symphonies and

Accompaniments
BY
SIR JOHN STEVENSON Mus Doc.

and Characteristic Words by

Thomas Moore Esq.

DUBLIN, Printed & Sold at W. Power's Music Warehouse, 4 Westmoreland Street, and at J. Power's Music & Instrument Warehouse 34. Strand, LONDON.

Price 15s British.
Ent.d at Stationers Hall

Songs of Love and Loss

The Young May Moon

This lilting serenade, like several of the other *Irish Melodies*, was originally composed by Turlough O'Carolan (1670–1738). O'Carolan has been styled "the last of the bards," for he combined the three offices of poet, harper and composer. In reality, he lived the life of a musical "traveling salesman," playing and sometimes composing airs such as this in honor of a patron who had given him a few nights' hospitality. The lyrical grace of "The Young May Moon" would not be out of place in the operas of Mozart or Rossini, but one can perhaps best imagine it sung by Moore himself in the candlelit ambience of a great eighteenth-century house.

> The young May moon is beaming, love,
> The glowworm's lamp is gleaming, love.
> How sweet to rove
> Thro' Morna's grove,
> While the drowsy world is dreaming, love!
> Then awake! The heavens look bright, my dear,
> 'Tis never too late for delight, my dear,
> And the best of all ways
> To lengthen our days,
> Is to steal a few hours from the night, my dear!
>
> Now all the world is sleeping, love,
> But the Sage, his star-watch keeping, love,
> And I whose star,
> More glorious far,
> Is the eye from that casement peeping, love.

Then awake!—till rise of sun, my dear,
The Sage's glass we'll shun, my dear,
Or, in watching the flight
Of bodies of light,
He might happen to take thee for one, my dear.

Oh! 'Tis Sweet to Think

It may be hard to believe, but Moore was attacked as a young man for "the vile and vulgar sensuality" of his romantic verses. In publishing this song Moore took pains to note that their praise of inconstancy should not be interpreted as "the actual and genuine sentiments of him who writes them."

Oh! 'tis sweet to think that, where'er we rove,
We are sure to find something blissful and dear,
And that, when we're far from the lips we love,
We have but to make love to the lips we are near!
The heart, like a tendril, accustom'd to cling,
Let it grow where it will, cannot flourish alone,
But will lean to the nearest and loveliest thing
It can twine with itself, and make closely its own.
Then, oh! what pleasure, where'er we rove,
To be doom'd to find something still that is dear;
And to know, when far from the lips we love,
We have but to make love to the lips we are near!

'Twere a shame, when flowers around us rise,
To make light of the rest if the rose is not there,
And the world's so rich in resplendent eyes,
'Twere a pity to limit one's love to a pair.
Love's wing and the peacock's are nearly alike,
They are both of them bright, but they're changeable too;
And, wherever a new beam of beauty can strike,
It will tincture Love's plume with a different hue.
Then, oh! what pleasure, where'er we rove,
To be doom'd to find something still that is dear;
And to know, when far from the lips we love,
We have but to make love to the lips we are near!

Echo

This eighteenth-century air was considerably arranged by Moore, including the introduction of two echo effects in the accompaniment. In its purity, simplicity and elegance, the piece reminds one of that other master of song, Franz Schubert.

How sweet the answer Echo makes
To music at night,
When, roused by lute or horn, she wakes, she starting wakes,
And far away, o'er lawns and lakes,
Goes answering light.

Yet Love hath echoes truer far,
And far more sweet,
Than e'er beneath the moonlight's star
Of horn, or lute, or soft guitar,
The songs repeat.

'Tis when the sigh, in youth sincere,
And only then,
The sigh, that's breathed for one to hear,
Is by that one, that only dear,
Breathed back again.

Lesbia Hath a Beaming Eye

Here Moore contrasts the innocence and charm of a simple Irish maiden with the artificial glitter of an English society belle. These same sentiments were formulated by much cruder writers associated with the Young Ireland movement into a political code whereby the alleged purity of the Irish peasantry was contrasted with the decadence of England.

Lesbia hath a beaming eye,
But no one knows for whom it beameth;
Right and left its arrows fly,
But what they aim at, no one dreameth.
Sweeter 'tis to gaze upon
My Nora's lid that seldom rises;
Few its looks but every one,
Like unexpected light, surprises.
Oh, my Nora Creina dear!
My gentle, bashful Nora Creina!
Beauty lies
In many eyes,
But Love in yours, my Nora Creina!

Lesbia wears a robe of gold,
But all so close the nymph hath lac'd it,
Not a charm of beauty's mould
Presumes to stay where nature placed it.
Oh! my Nora's gown for me,
That floats as wild as mountain breezes,
Leaving ev'ry beauty free

To sink or swell as heaven pleases.
Yes, my Nora Creina dear,
My simple, graceful Nora Creina!
Nature's dress,
Is loveliness—
The dress you wear, my Nora Creina!

Lesbia hath a wit refin'd,
But, when its points are gleaming round
    us,
Who can tell if they're designed
To dazzle merely, or to wound us?
Pillow'd on my Nora's heart,
In safer slumber love reposes—
Bed of peace! whose roughest part
Is but the crumpling of the roses.
Oh, my Nora Creina dear!
My mild, my artless Nora Creina!
Wit, though bright,
Hath no such light,
As warms your eyes, my Nora Creina!

I've a Secret to Tell Thee

The reference in the second stanza is to Harsiesis, known as the Egyptian god of discretion from depictions of him as a child sucking his thumb. Like many other writers of the time, Moore was fascinated by the mythology of the Middle East, finding in it many parallels with the Celtic tradition.

I've a secret to tell thee, but, hush! not here,
Oh! not where the world its vigil keeps:
I'll seek to whisper it in thine ear,
Some shore where the Spirit of Silence sleeps;
Where summer's wave unmurm'ring dies,
Nor fay can hear the fountain's gush;
Where, if but a note her nightbird sighs,
The Rose saith, chidingly, "Hush, sweet, hush!"

There, 'mid the deep silence of that hour
When stars can be heard in ocean dip,
Thyself shall, under some rosy bow'r,
Sit mute, with thy finger on thy lip:
Like him, the boy, who born among
The flowers that on the Nile-stream blush,
Sits ever thus, his only song
To earth and heaven, "Hush, all hush!"

They Know Not My Heart

In its exaltation of a spiritualized love for an ideal beauty, the lyric reminds one of the courtly love songs of the mediaeval troubadours. Here, as elsewhere in Moore, there is a ravishing liquid flow to the lines that sets up the suspended high notes—a perfect wedding of sound to feeling.

They know not my heart, who believe there can be
One stain of this earth in its feelings for thee;
Who think, while I see thee in beauty's young hour,
As pure as the morning's first dew on the flow'r,
I could harm what I love as the sun's wanton ray
But smiles on the dewdrop to waste it away!

No, beaming with light as those young features are,
There's a light round thy heart which is lovelier far;
It is not that cheek, 'tis the soul dawning clear
Thro' its innocent blush makes thy beauty so dear;
As the sky we look up to, though glorious and fair,
Is look'd up to the more, because heaven lies there!

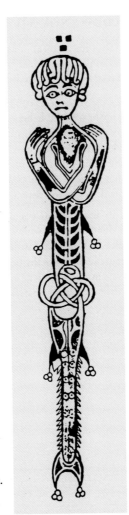

Mermaid from the Book of Kells.

Has Sorrow Thy Young Days Shaded

This lyric may be interpreted either as a gesture of solace towards a suffering loved one or as an allegory of Ireland's misfortune. Moore explains that the Lagenian mine in the second stanza refers to Wicklow gold mines—which deserve the quixotic character here given of them. Another image of evanescent hope, the bird that steals a pen from the talisman and then mocks him by flying with it just out of reach, comes from Moore's reading of *The Arabian Nights*.

Has sorrow thy young days shaded,
As clouds o'er the morning fleet?
Too fast have those young days faded,
That, even in sorrow, were sweet?
Does Time with his cold wing wither
Each feeling that once was dear?
Then, child of misfortune, come hither,
I'll weep with thee, tear for tear.

Has love to that soul, so tender,
Been like our Lagenian mine,
Where sparkles of golden splendour
All over the surface shine?
But, if in pursuit we go deeper,
Allured by the gleam that shone,
Ah! false as the dream of the sleeper,
Like Love, the bright ore is gone.

Has Hope, like the bird in the story,
That flitted from tree to tree
With the talisman's glittering glory
Has hope been that bird to thee?
On branch after branch alighting
The gem did she still display,
And, when nearest and most inviting,
Then waft the fair gem away?

If thus the young hours have fleeted
When sorrow itself look'd bright;
If thus the fair hope hath cheated
That led thee along so light;
If thus the cold world now wither
Each feeling that once was dear:
Come, child of misfortune, come hither,
I'll weep with thee, tear for tear.

Believe Me, If All Those Endearing Young Charms

It is said that this exquisite ode to the enduring power of love was intended to ease the anguish of the wife of the Duke of Wellington when she was afflicted with disfiguring smallpox. One of the most popular of all Moore's airs, it was sung on three occasions by Inspector Bucket in Dickens's *Bleak House* as a reminder of how he has won his wife's hand. The song was also featured in a 1951 Warner Brothers cartoon called "Ballot Box Bunny" which starred Bugs Bunny and Yosemite Sam! The air itself was borrowed for "Fair Harvard"—the anthem of Harvard University—an example of the huge influence Moore had on nineteenth-century American music.

> Believe me, if all those endearing young charms,
> Which I gaze on so fondly today,
> Were to change by tomorrow, and fleet in my arms,
> Like fairy gifts fading away;—
> Thou wouldst still be ador'd, as this moment thou art,
> Let thy loveliness fade as it will;—
> And around the dear ruin each wish of my heart
> Would entwine itself verdantly still.
>
> It is not while beauty and youth are thine own,
> And thy cheeks unprofan'd by a tear,—
> That the fervour and faith of a soul can be known,
> To which time will but make thee more dear!
> Oh, the heart, that has truly lov'd, never forgets,
> But as truly loves on to the close;—
> As the sunflower turns on her god, when he sets,
> The same look which she turn'd when he rose.

How Dear to Me

Written to an ancient pentatonic air, the lyrics evoke an idyllic isle of escape—*Tir-na-n Òg*, the Land of Eternal Youth—lying beyond the Western sea.

How dear to me the hour when daylight dies,
And sunbeams melt along the silent sea,
For then sweet dreams of other days arise,
And Mem'ry breathes her vesper sigh to thee.

And as I watch the line of light that plays,
Along the smooth wave, tow'rds the burning West,
I long to tread that golden path of rays,
And think 'twould lead to some bright isle of rest.

'Tis the Last Rose of Summer

The words and music of this famous song were quoted verbatim by Friedrich von Flotow in the second act of his opera *Martha* (1847), a sign not only of Moore's popularity but also of his contribution to the widespread interest in Celtic and especially Irish material. The last stanza evokes, with a prophetic poignancy, the loneliness of Moore's own declining years when all that was left to him was the solace of his beloved wife, Bessie.

'Tis the last rose of summer
Left blooming alone;
All her lovely companions
Are faded and gone;
No flower of her kindred,
No rose-bud is nigh,
To reflect back her blushes,
Or give sigh for sigh.

I'll not leave thee, thou lone one,
To pine on the stem;
Since the lovely are sleeping,
Go, sleep thou with them.
Thus kindly I scatter
Thy leaves o'er the bed,
Where thy mates of the garden
Lie scentless and dead.

So soon may I follow,
When friendships decay,
And from love's shining circle
The gems drop away.
When true hearts lie wither'd,
And fond ones are flown,
Oh! who would inhabit
This bleak world alone?

O'Donoghue's Mistress

Legend has it that every year on the first of May the ghost of the Chieftain O'Donoghue returns to glide over the waters of Lake Killarney on his favorite white horse. His grieving mistress promises that one day she will throw herself into the waters to join him in death.

Of all the fair months that round the Sun
In light-link'd dance their circles run,
Sweet May, sweet May, shine thou for me,
Sweet May, shine thou for me;
For still when thy earliest beams arise,
That Youth, who beneath the blue lake lies,
Sweet May, sweet May, returns to me,
Sweet May, returns to me.

Of all the proud steeds, that ever bore
Young plumèd chiefs on sea or shore,
White steed, white steed, most joy to thee,
White steed, most joy to thee;
Who still, with the first young glance of spring,
From under that glorious lake dost bring
My love, my chief, to me.

Of all the sweet deaths that maidens die,
Whose lovers beneath the cold wave lie,
Most sweet, most sweet, that death will be,
Most sweet that death will be,
Which under the next May evening's light,
When thou and thy steed are lost to sight,
Dear love, dear love, I'll die for thee,
Dear love, I'll die for thee.

The Meeting of the Waters

Moore's very Irish feeling for "good *craic*," or the convivial moment, is seen in this song inspired by a visit to the beauteous Vale of Avoca in the company of friends. James Joyce made many references to the song, including one in *Ulysses* where Leopold Bloom remarks, *à propos* of the ugly statue of Moore in College Green, Dublin: "They did right to put him up over a urinal: meeting of the waters."

There is not in the wide world a valley so sweet
As that vale in whose bosom the bright waters meet;
Oh! the last rays of feeling and life must depart,
Ere the bloom of that valley shall fade from my heart!

Yet it was not that Nature had shed o'er the scene
Her purest of crystal and brightest of green;
'Twas not her soft magic of streamlet or hill,
Oh! no—it was something more exquisite still.

'Twas that friends, the beloved of my bosom, were near,
Who made every dear scene of enchantment more dear,
And who felt how the best charms of Nature improve
When we see them reflected from looks that we love,

Sweet vale of Avoca! how calm could I rest
In thy bosom of shade, with the friends I love best,
Where the storms that we feel in this cold world should cease,
And our hearts, like thy waters, be mingled in peace.

The Meeting of the Waters *by R. Wallace after T. Creswick, 1856.*

They May Rail at This Life

Based upon an eighteenth-century dance tune, this rollicking love song displays Moore's high spirits, comic flair and verbal agility at their best. In its broad popular style it also anticipates the musical hall ballads of Irish songwriters like Percy French (1854–1920). Above all, however, one is aware of Moore the performer, roguishly teasing and flirting with his audience, while transporting them on planetary flights—and beyond . . .

They may rail at this life from the hour I began it,
I've found it a life full of kindness and bliss;
And until they can show me some happier planet,
More social and bright, I'll content me with this.
As long as the world has such eloquent eyes,
As before me this moment enraptur'd I see,
They may say what they will of their orbs in the skies,
But this earth is the planet for you, love, and me.

In Mercury's star, where each minute can bring them
New sunshine and wit from the fountain on high,
Tho' the Nymphs may have livelier poets to sing them,
They've none, even there, more enamour'd than I.
And, as long as this harp can be waken'd to love,
And that eye its divine inspiration shall be,
They may talk as they will of their Edens above,
But this earth is the planet for you, love, and me.

In that star of the west, by whose shadowy splendour,
At twilight so often we've roam'd through the dew,
There are maidens, perhaps, who have bosoms as tender,
And look, in their twilights, as lovely as you.

But, though they were even more bright than the queen
of that isle they inhabit in heaven's blue sea,
As I never these fair young celestials have seen,
Why,—this earth is the planet for you, love, and me.

As for those chilly orbs on the verge of creation,
Where sunshine and smiles must be equally rare,
Did they want a supply of cold hearts for that station,
Heaven knows, we have plenty on earth we could spare.
Oh, think what a world we should have of it here,
If the haters of peace, of affection, and glee,
Were to fly up to Saturn's comfortless sphere,
And leave earth to such spirits as you, love, and me.

Come, Send Round the Wine

This extraordinary plea for religious tolerance is consistent with Moore's lifelong battle against English laws that imposed massive restrictions on the rights of his fellow Irish Catholics. "The heretic girl" referred to in the second stanza is Moore's wife, Bessie, herself a Protestant, whom he married in 1811.

Come, send round the wine, and leave points of belief
To simpleton sages and reas'ning fools;
This moment's a flow'r too fair and too brief,
To be wither'd and stain'd by the dust of the schools.
Your glass may be purple and mine may be blue,
But while they're both fill'd from the same bright bowl,
The fool that would quarrel for difference of hue,
Deserves not the comfort they shed o'er the soul.

Shall I ask the brave soldier who fights by my side
In the cause of mankind, if our creeds agree?
Shall I give up the friend I have valued and tried,
If he kneel not before the same altar with me?
From the heretic girl of my soul should I fly,
To seek somewhere else a more orthodox kiss?
No, perish the hearts, and the laws that try
Truth, valour, or love, by a standard like this!

Farewell! But, Whene'er You Welcome the Hour

Moore had a genius for friendship. Byron, who described him as the most pleasing individual he had ever met, begged for his companionship when in exile, knew his songs by heart and often quoted them in his correspondence. In turn, Moore reveled in the company of others as much as they in his, as evident in this touching threnody on the sadness of separation from those one loves.

Farewell! but, whene'er you welcome the
   hour,
Which awakens the nightsong of mirth
   in your bower,
Then think of the friend, who once
   welcomed it too,
And forgot his own griefs to be happy
   with you.
His griefs may return, not a hope may
   remain
Of the few that have brighten'd his
   pathway of pain,
But he ne'er will forget the short vision
   that threw
Its enchantment around him, while
   ling'ring with you!

And still on that evening when pleasure
   fills up
To the highest top sparkle each heart
   and each cup,
Where'er my path lies, be it gloomy or
   bright,
My soul, happy friends, shall be with you
   that night;

Shall join in your revels, your sports, and
   your wiles,
And return to me beaming all o'er with
   your smiles—
Too blest, if it tells me, that 'mid the gay
   cheer,
Some kind voice had murmur'd, "I wish
   he were here!"

Let Fate do her worst, there are relics of
   joy,
Bright dreams of the past, which she
   cannot destroy;
Which come in the night-time of sorrow
   and care,
And bring back the features that joy
   used to wear.
Long, long be my heart with such
   memories fill'd!
Like the vase, in which roses have once
   been distill'd—
You may break, you may shatter the vase
   if you will,
But the scent of the roses will hang
   round it still.

Whene'er I See Those Smiling Eyes

No more moving passage in all of Moore's work exists than the description from his 1829 *Journal* of the death from tuberculosis of his fourteen-year-old daughter, Anastasia. Afterward, the very thought of her caused him to be seized with violent sobbing fits. It is easy to imagine that this song held a sad premonition for Moore.

Whene'er I see those smiling eyes,
So full of hope, and joy, and light,
As if no cloud could ever rise,
To dim a heav'n so purely bright;
I sigh to think how soon that brow
In grief may lose its ev'ry ray,
And that light heart, so joyous now,
Almost forget it once was gay.

For time will come with all its blights,
The ruin'd hope, the friend unkind,
And love, that leaves, where'er it lights,
A chill'd or burning heart behind;
While youth, that now like snow appears,
Ere sullied by the dark'ning rain,
When once 'tis touch'd by sorrow's tears
Will never shine so bright again.

Oh! Arranmore, Loved Arranmore

Arranmore is an island lying nine miles off the northwest coast of Ireland. In Moore's time the inhabitants of the island were persuaded that on a clear day they could see the paradise of *Tir-na-n Òg* beyond the western horizon.

Oh! Arranmore, loved Arranmore,
How oft I dream of thee,
And of those days when, by thy shore,
I wander'd young and free.
Full many a path I've tried, since then,
Through pleasure's flow'ry maze,
But ne'er could find the bliss again
I felt in those sweet days.

How blithe upon thy breezy cliffs
At sunny morn I've stood,
With heart as bounding as the skiffs
That danc'd along thy flood;
Or, when the Western wave grew bright
With daylight's parting wing,
Have sought that Eden in its light
Which dreaming poets sing;

That Eden where th' immortal brave
Dwell in a land serene,
Whose bowers beyond the shining wave,
At sunset, oft are seen.
Ah dream too full of sadd'ning truth!
Those mansions o'er the main
Are like the hopes I built in youth,
As sunny and as vain!

At the Mid Hour of Night

"In Ireland this world and the world we go to after death are not far apart," wrote Yeats in *The Celtic Twilight*. This lyric perfectly illustrates that idea, which is probably why it and "Oft in the Stilly Night" were so admired by him.

At the mid hour of night, when stars are weeping, I fly
To the lone vale we lov'd, when life shone warm in thine eye;
And I think that, if spirits can steal from the region of air
To revisit past scenes of delight, thou wilt come to me there,
And tell me our love is remember'd even in the sky!

Then I sing the wild song, which once 'twas pleasure to hear,
When our voices, commingling, breath'd like one on the ear;
And, as Echo far off through the vale my sad orison rolls,
I think, oh my love! 'tis thy voice from the kingdom of souls,
Faintly answering still the notes that once were so dear!

Oft in the Stilly Night

This air takes on a special meaning when one considers the tragedy of Moore's final days: an exile, bereft of the comfort of his children and friends, with even his integrity called into question by many of those who had once idolized him.

Oft in the stilly night,
Ere slumber's chain has bound me,
Fond mem'ry brings the light
Of other days around me;
The smiles, the tears of boyhood's years,
The words of love then spoken,
The eyes that shone now dim'd and gone,
The cheerful hearts now broken!
Thus, in the stilly night,
Ere slumber's chain has bound me,
Sad mem'ry brings the light
Of other days around me.

When I remember all
The friends, so link'd together,
I've seen around me fall,
Like leaves in wintry weather;
I feel like one who treads alone
Some banquet hall deserted,
Whose lights are fled, whose garlands dead,
And all but he departed!
Thus, in the stilly night,
Ere slumber's chain has bound me,
Sad mem'ry brings the light
Of other days around me.

Songs of Romance and Rebellion

The Harp That Once Through Tara's Halls

Once the site of pagan ceremonies in honor of the goddess Maeve, the Hill of Tara later housed the so-called High Kings of Ireland in a palace of legendary splendor. It was at Tara that in the year 432 A.D. St. Patrick is said to have begun his successful crusade to convert the heathen Irish to Christianity. To Thomas Moore, there could be no more appropriate symbol of the destruction of Gaelic Ireland than the harp of Tara hung mute upon a barren wall. Tara, of course, also provided another now-legendary image of destruction in the film *Gone With the Wind*.

> The Harp that once through Tara's halls
> The soul of Music shed,
> Now hangs as mute on Tara's walls
> As if that soul were fled.
> So sleeps the pride of former days,
> So glory's thrill is o'er;
> And hearts, that once beat high for praise,
> Now feel that pulse no more.
>
> No more to chiefs and ladies bright
> The harp of Tara swells;
> The chord, alone that breaks at night
> Its tale of ruin tells.
> Thus Freedom now so seldom wakes,
> The only throb she gives
> Is when some heart indignant breaks,
> To show that still she lives.

Silent, Oh Moyle

This lyric is based upon the legend of Fionnuala, the daughter of Lir, who was transformed into a swan by her jealous stepmother Aoife. In this disguise she was condemned to wander for hundreds of years over certain lakes and rivers until the coming of Christianity to Ireland when the sound of the Mass-bell would signal her release. Moore took this well-known Irish legend and turned it into a political allegory.

Silent, Oh Moyle, be the roar of thy water,—
Break not, ye breezes, your chain of repose;
While murmuring mournfully, Lir's lonely daughter
Tells to the night-star her tale of woes.
When shall the swan, her death-note singing,
Sleep with wings in darkness furl'd?
When shall heav'n, its sweet bell ringing,
Call my spirit from this stormy world?

Sadly, Oh Moyle, to thy winter-wave weeping,
Fate bids me languish long ages away;
Yet still in her darkness doth Erin lie sleeping,
Still doth the pure light its dawning delay!
When will that day-star, mildly springing,
Warm our Isle with peace and love?
When shall heav'n, its sweet bell ringing,
Call my spirit to the fields above?

Remember the Glories of Brien the Brave

Written to one of the oldest of the airs in Edward Bunting's *Collection of the Ancient Music of Ireland* (1796), this lyric commemorates the valor of Brien Boru (947–1014), the first High King of Ireland and thereby one of the earliest symbols of a unified Irish nation. Brien ruled Ireland from his palace at Kincora in the Province of Munster (Mononia) until his death at the Battle of Clontarf, which ended Viking power in Ireland. The third stanza refers to the favorite troops of Brien who, even though wounded, asked to be tied to stakes so as to continue fighting beside their comrades. Frank O'Connor credited his father's singing of this song with stirring in him for the first time a conscious realization of poetry.

Remember the glories of Brien the brave,
Tho' the days of the hero are o'er;
Tho' lost to Mononia and cold in the grave,
He returns to Kincora no more!
That star of the field, which so often has pour'd
Its beam on the battle, is set;
But enough of its glory remains on each sword
To light us to victory yet.

Mononia! when Nature embellish'd the tint
Of thy fields, and thy mountains so fair,
Did she ever intend that a tyrant should print
The footstep of slavery there?
No, Freedom, whose smile we shall never resign,
Go, tell our invaders, the Danes,
That 'tis sweeter to bleed for an age at thy shrine
Than to sleep but a moment in chains!

Forget not our wounded companions, who stood
In the day of distress by our side;
While the moss of the valley grew red with their blood,
They stirr'd not, but conquer'd and died!
The sun, that now blesses our arms with his light,
Saw them fall upon Ossory's plain;
Oh! let him not blush, when he leaves us tonight,
To find that they fell there in vain!

Come, Rest in This Bosom

This is Moore's version of an eighteenth-century poetic form, the *aisling*, or vision poem. In the *aisling* tradition Ireland is personified as a beautiful woman fleeing an unwanted foreign suitor while in search of her one true love—a love whom she will know by his willingness to endure any sacrifice, including death, for her sake. Yeats's revolutionary play, *Cathleen ni Houlihan*, is derived from the same source.

Come, rest in this bosom, my own stricken deer!
Tho' the herd have fled from thee, thy home is still here;
Here still is the smile that no cloud can o'ercast,
And the heart and the hand all thy own to the last!

Oh! what was love made for, if 'tis not the same
Through joy and through torment, through glory and shame?
I know not, I ask not, if guilt's in that heart,
I but know that I love thee, whatever thou art.

Thou has call'd me thy Angel in moments of bliss,
And thy Angel I'll be, 'mid the horrors of this,
Through the furnace, unshrinking, thy steps to pursue,
And shield thee, and save thee, or perish there too.

Oh! Breathe Not His Name

Moore wrote this lament in memory of his friend Robert Emmet. The exact site of Emmet's grave is not known; thus, appropriately, his epitaph still has not been written. The French composer Henri Duparc wrote a setting for this piece entitled "Élegie."

Oh! breathe not his name, let it sleep in the shade,
Where cold and unhonour'd his relics are laid;
Sad, silent, and dark, be the tears that we shed,
As the night dew that falls on the grass o'er his head.

But the night-dew that falls, though in silence it weeps,
Shall brighten with verdure the grave where he sleeps;
And the tear that we shed, though in secret it rolls,
Shall long keep his memory green in our souls.

She Is Far from the Land

This song commemorates the memory of Emmet's sweetheart, Sarah Curran (1783–1808), who, after his execution, went into exile, dying, it is said, from a broken heart. Joxer Boyle performs a halting version of this piece in the second act party scene of Sean O'Casey's *Juno and the Paycock*. Samuel Beckett draws upon the social and historical imagery of the song only to parody its nationalist sentiment in *The Unnamable*.

She is far from the land where her young hero sleeps,
And lovers are 'round her sighing;
But coldly she turns from their gaze, and weeps,
For her heart in his grave is lying!

She sings the wild songs of her dear native plains,
Every note which he loved awaking;
Ah! little they think, who delight in her strains,
How the heart of the Minstrel is breaking.

He had lived for his love, for his country he died,
They were all that to life had entwined him;
Nor soon shall the tears of his country be dried,
Nor long will his love stay behind him.

Oh! make her a grave where the sunbeams rest
When they promise a glorious morrow;
They'll shine o'er her sleep, like a smile from the West,
From her own lov'd island of sorrow.

When He Who Adores Thee

This bittersweet love song is addressed to Ireland by Lord Edward Fitzgerald. "Though the Last Glimpse of Erin" and this were, understandably, Byron's two favorites from among the Moore *Melodies*.

When he who adores thee has left but the name
Of his fault and his sorrow behind,
Oh! say, wilt thou weep when they darken the fame
Of a life that for thee was resign'd?
Yes, weep! and, however my foes may condemn,
Thy tears shall efface their decree;
For Heav'n can witness, though guilty to them,
I have been but too faithful to thee!

With thee were the dreams of my earliest love,
Every thought of my reason was thine:
In my last humble pray'r to the Spirit above,
Thy name shall be mingled with mine!
Oh! bless'd are the lovers and friends who shall live
The days of thy glory to see;
But the next dearest blessing that heaven can give
Is the pride of thus dying for thee!

Portrait of Lord Edward Fitzgerald by Hugh Douglas Hamilton, 1796.

Oh! Ye Dead!

A dirge set to an ancient air in which, according to Irish folk belief, the shadows of men who have died on foreign soil will return to haunt dearly beloved places. "Oh! Ye Dead!" was one of the favorite songs of Joyce and one of the inspirations for his brilliant short story, "The Dead."

Oh, ye Dead! Oh, ye Dead! whom we know by the light you give
From your cold gleaming eyes,
Though you move like men who live;
Why leave you thus your graves,
In far off fields and waves,
Where the worm and the seabird only know your bed,
To haunt this spot, where all
Those eyes that wept your fall,
And the hearts that bewail'd you, like your own, lie dead?

It is true, it is true, we are shadows cold and wan;
And the fair and the brave whom we lov'd on earth are gone;
But still, thus ev'n in death,
So sweet the living breath
Of the fields and the flow'rs in our youth we wander'd o'er,
That ere, condemn'd, we go
To freeze 'mid Hecla's snow.
We would taste it awhile, and think we live once more!

I Wish I Was by That Dim Lake

An ancient melody with lyrics that evoke St. Patrick's Purgatory at Station Island in Lough Derg, County Donegal. Associated with the Saint for 1,500 years, pilgrims still gather for three rigorous days of penitential fasting, hoping to win pardon for their sins. The title poem of Seamus Heaney's collection *Station Island* (1979) transforms this pilgrimage into an inner journey to find the forces necessary to face the crises of the modern world.

I wish I was by that dim lake,
Where sinful souls their farewell take
Of this vain world, and halfway lie
In death's cold shadow, ere they die.
There, there, far from thee,
Deceitful world, my home should be—
Where, come what might of gloom and
    pain,
False hope should ne'er deceive again!

The lifeless sky, the mournful sound
Of unseen waters, falling round—
The dry leaves quiv'ring o'er my head,
Like man, unquiet ev'n when dead—
These, ay, these should wean
My soul from life's deluding scene,
And turn each thought, each wish I have,
Like willows, downward tow'rds the
    grave.

As they, who to their couch at night
Would welcome sleep, first quench the
    light,
So must the hopes, that keep this breast
Awake, be quench'd, ere it can rest.
Cold, cold, my heart must grow,
Unchanged by either joy or woe,
Like freezing founts, where all that's
    thrown
Within their current turns to stone.

Let Erin Remember

Malachi, a tenth-century king of the northern half of Ireland, was famed for defeating two Viking champions in hand-to-hand combat, from one of which he took a collar of gold, or *torc*. The Red Branch Knights of Ulster were said to have been established before the birth of Christ. Round towers beneath Lough Neagh's waters stem from an old tradition that the Lough was originally a fountain whose sudden overflowing inundated the whole countryside, like Plato's Atlantis. In re-invoking these images, Moore believed, as did Yeats, that their latent power could re-animate the patriotism of his fellow countrymen.

> Let Erin remember the days of old,
> Ere her faithless sons betray'd her,
> When Malachi wore the collar of gold,
> Which he won from her proud invader;
> When her Kings, with standard of green unfurl'd,
> Led the Red-Branch Knights to danger,
> Ere the em'rald gem of the western world
> Was set in the crown of a stranger.
>
> On Lough-Neagh's bank, as the fisherman strays,
> When the clear cold eve's declining,
> He sees the round towers of other days
> In the wave beneath him shining!
> Thus shall Memory often, in dreams sublime,
> Catch a glimpse of the days that are over;
> Thus, sighing, look through the waves of Time
> For the long-faded glories they cover!

Avenging and Bright

This stirring battle song is based upon the legendary betrayal of Deirdre and the sons of Usna by Conchubar, the King of Ulster. There can be no mistaking the real object of Moore's wrath, however. In 1811, the year when the air was published, Moore broke with his friend and patron, the Prince of Wales (soon to be George IV), when, upon becoming Regent, the Prince betrayed the cause of Catholic Emancipation.

Avenging and bright fall the swift sword of Erin,
On him, who the brave sons of Usna betray'd;
For ev'ry fond eye which he waken'd a tear in,
A drop from his heart-wounds shall weep o'er her blade.

By the red cloud that hung over Conor's dark dwelling,
When Ulad's three champions lay sleeping in gore—
By the billows of war, which so often, high swelling,
Have wafted these heroes to victory's shore.

We swear to revenge them!—no joy shall be tasted,
The harp shall be silent, the maiden unwed,
Our halls shall be mute and our fields shall lie wasted,
Till vengeance is wreak'd on the murderer's head!

Yes, monarch! though sweet are our home recollections,
Though sweet are the tears that from tenderness fall;
Though sweet are our friendships, our hopes, our affections,
Revenge on a tyrant is sweetest of all!

The Minstrel Boy

In this song Moore invokes the age-old idea of the minstrel as a symbol of Ireland's national identity. Joyce often quoted in mockery from "The Minstrel Boy" while Shaw and O'Casey parodied its patriotic theme in *John Bull's Other Island* and *The Plough and the Stars*, respectively. On the other hand, Yeats echoed Moore's own views on intellectual freedom when he championed the plays of Synge and O'Casey against those misguided patriots who tried to suppress them at the Abbey Theatre.

> The Minstrel Boy to the war is gone,
> In the ranks of death you'll find him;
> His father's sword he has girded on,
> And his wild harp slung behind him.
> "Land of song!" said the warrior-bard,
> "Tho' all the world betrays thee,
> "One sword, at least, thy rights shall guard,
> "One faithful harp shall praise thee!"
>
> The Minstrel fell!—but the foeman's chain
> Could not bring that proud soul under;
> The harp he lov'd never spoke again,
> For he tore its chords asunder;
> And said, "No chains shall sully thee,
> "Thou soul of love and bravery!
> "Thy songs were made for the pure and free,
> "They shall never sound in slavery."

As Vanquish'd Erin

This song leaps three centuries from the July 1690 Battle of the Boyne, which marked the final defeat of Catholic Gaelic Ireland, to the annual commemoration of that defeat on the "madd'ning" streets of contemporary Belfast. The bitterly ironic images of the song are all the more telling when one realizes that the air is still employed as the marching song of the Orange Order of Northern Ireland.

As vanquish'd Erin wept beside
The Boyne's ill-fated river,
She saw where Discord, in the tide,
Had dropp'd his loaded quiver.
"Lie hid," she cried, "ye venom'd darts,
Where mortal eye may shun you,
Lie hid for oh! the stain of hearts
That bled for me is on you."

But vain her wish, her weeping vain,
As Time too well hath taught her,
Each year the Fiend returns again,
And dives into that water;
And brings, triumphant, from beneath
His shafts of desolation,
And sends them, wing'd with worse than
   death,
Through all her madd'ning nation.

Alas for her who sits and mourns,
Ev'n now, beside that river!
Unwearied still the fiend returns,
And stor'd is still his quiver.
"When will this end, ye Powers of
   Good?"
She weeping asks for ever;
But only hears, from out that flood,
The Demon answer, "Never!"

Manuscript of Thomas Moore's "The Fortune Teller."

The Irish Peasant to His Mistress

Augustine Martin comments on this lyric: "The Irish countryman's bond with his Church is portrayed as mystically as Red Hanraham's communion with the Shee in the early Yeats. Given a substantial theme Moore's imagery of the crown of thorns, the catacombs, and the Mass rock struck shrewdly at the conscience of the times. The poem's last stanza, where he equates liberty with the spirit of Catholicism, must have been more than mildly provocative to contemporary sensibilities."

Thro' grief and thro' danger thy smile hath cheer'd my way,
Till hope seem'd to bud from each thorn, that round me lay;
The darker our fortune, the brighter our pure love burned,
Till shame into glory, till fear into zeal was turn'd;
Yet! slave as I was, in thy arms my spirit felt free,
And bless'd ev'n the sorrows that made me more dear to thee.

Thy rival was honour'd, whilst thou wert wrong'd and scorn'd,
Thy crown was of briers, while gold her brows adorn'd;
She woo'd me to temples, while thou layest hid in caves,
Her friends were all masters, while thine, alas! were slaves;
Yet cold in the earth, at thy feet, I would rather be,
Than wed what I love not, or turn one thought from thee.

They slander thee sorely, who say thy vows are frail—
Hadst thou been a false one, thy cheek had look'd less pale.
They say, too, so long thou hast worn those ling'ring chains,
That deep in thy heart they have printed their servile stains—
Oh! foul is the slander, no chain could that soul subdue—
Where shineth thy spirit, there liberty shineth too!

Oh, Banquet Not

Moore here adapted a bright, bouncing *planxty*, or song of praise for a noble patron, so as to provide it with a new meaning that underscores Ireland's tragic history. The dramatic tension between the happy associations of the air and the bitter images of Moore's lyric anticipated the deliberately contradictory effect achieved in the satiric songs of Bertolt Brecht and Kurt Weill.

Oh, banquet not in those shining bowers
Where Youth resorts, but come to me;
For mine's a garden of faded flowers,
More fit for sorrow, for age, and thee.
And there we shall have our feast of tears,
And many a cup in silence pour
Our guests the shades of former years,
Our toasts to lips that bloom no more.

There, while the myrtle's withering boughs
Their lifeless leaves around us shed,
We'll brim the bowl to broken vows,
To friends long lost, the changed, the dead!
Or, while some blighted laurel waves
Its branches o'er the dreary spot,
We'll drink to those neglected graves,
Where Valour sleeps, unnamed, forgot.

Come O'er the Sea

The theme of exile is obviously one for which Moore had deep feeling. As he once wrote to his friend and patron, Her Ladyship, the Marchioness Dowager of Donegal: "Absence, however fatal to some affections of the heart, rather strengthens our love for the land where we were born; and Ireland is the country, of all others, which an exile from it must remember with most enthusiasm. Those few darker and less amiable traits with which bigotry and misrule have stained her character, and which are apt to disgust us upon a nearer intercourse, become softened at a distance, or altogether invisible; and nothing is remembered but her virtues and her misfortunes—the ease with which her generous spirit might be conciliated, and the cruel ingenuity which has been exerted to 'Wring her into undutifulness.'"

Come o'er the sea,
Maiden, with me,
Mine thro' sunshine, storm and
    snows;
Seasons may roll,
But the true soul
Burns the same, where'er it goes.
Let Fate frown on, so we love and
    part not;
'Tis life where thou art, 'tis death
    where thou art not.
Then come o'er the Sea,
Maiden, with me,
Come wherever the wild wind blows;
Seasons may roll,
But the true soul
Burns the same, wherever it goes.

Was not the sea
Made for the free,
Land for courts and chains alone?
Here we are slaves,
But, on the waves,
Love and liberty's all our own.
No eye to watch, and no tongue to
    wound us,
All earth forgot, and all heaven around
    us.
Then, come o'er the sea,
Maiden, with me,
Mine through sunshine, storm, and
    snows;
Seasons may roll,
But the true soul
Burns the same, where'er it goes.

Though the Last Glimpse of Erin

To one of the great airs in the Gaelic tradition Moore wrote a lyric from the standpoint of a young woman who chooses to follow her beloved into exile rather than allow him to suffer the humility of continued oppression. The song is based upon a law enacted in the reign of Henry VIII which prohibited Irish males from wearing moustaches or *coulins* (long locks) on their heads. That archetypal Irish exile, James Joyce, dedicated an autobiographical note to his Galway-born wife, Nora, by quoting the second line of the song.

Tho' the last glimpse of Erin with sorrow I see,
Yet wherever thou art shall seem Erin to me;
In exile thy bosom shall still be my home,
And thine eyes make my climate wherever we roam.

To the gloom of some desert, or cold rocky shore,
Where the eye of the stranger can haunt us no more,
I will fly with my Coulin, and think the rough wind
Less rude than the foes we leave frowning behind.

And I'll gaze on thy gold hair, as graceful it wreathes,
And hang o'er thy soft harp, as wildly it breathes;
Nor dread that the cold-hearted Saxon may tear
One chord from that harp, or one lock from that hair.

Sweet Innisfallen

Inisfallen, a lovely island in the middle of Lake Killarney, provided Moore with an exquisite memory to hold in exile. In turn, Moore's song provided another exile, Sean O'Casey, with the title of one of his autobiographies.

Sweet Innisfallen, fare thee well,
May calm and sunshine long be thine!
How fair thou art let others tell—
To feel how fair shall long be mine.

Sweet Innisfallen, long shall dwell
In memory's dream that sunny smile,
Which o'er thee on that evening fell—
When first I saw thy fairy isle.

No more along thy shores to come,
But, on the world's rude ocean tost,
Dream of thee sometimes, as a home
Of sunshine he had seen and lost!

Weeping or smiling, lovely isle!
And all the lovelier for thy tears—
For though but rare thy sunny smile,
'Tis Heaven's own glance, when it appears.

Like feeling hearts, whose joys are few,
But, when indeed they come, divine—
The brightest light the sun e'er threw
Is lifeless to one gleam of thine!

Dear Harp of My Country

Intended to be Moore's farewell to music, this song, published in 1815, avows that in all he wrought the poet was only a vessel of Ireland's genius.

Dear Harp of my Country! in darkness I found thee,
The cold chain of silence had hung o'er thee long,
When proudly, my own island Harp! I unbound thee,
And gave all thy chords to light, freedom and song!
The warm lay of love and the light note of gladness
Have waken'd thy fondest, thy liveliest thrill;
But so oft hast thou echo'd the deep sigh of sadness
That ev'n in thy mirth it will steal from thee still.

Dear Harp of my Country! farewell to thy numbers,
This sweet wreath of song is the last we shall twine;
Go, sleep, with the sunshine of Fame on thy slumbers,
Till touch'd by some hand less unworthy than mine.
If the pulse of the patriot, soldier, or lover,
Have throbb'd at our lay, 'tis thy glory alone;
It was but as the wind, passing heedlessly over,
And all the wild sweetness I waked was thy own!

Erin! The Tear and the Smile in Thine Eyes

The theme of this song, a plea for an end to Ireland's tragic disunity, is as relevant today as it was when Moore first penned it.

Erin, the tear and the smile in thine eyes
Blend like the rainbow that hangs in the skies;
Shining through sorrow's stream,
Sadd'ning through pleasure's beam,
Thy suns, with doubtful gleam,
Weep while they rise!

Erin, thy silent tear never shall cease,
Erin, thy languid smile ne'er shall increase,
Till, like the rainbow's light,
Thy various tints unite,
And form in Heaven's sight
One arch of peace!

Afterword

Were he alive now, Thomas Moore would be considered a mega-star. His were the days of sheet music, but he had an impact on Ireland, Europe and America which in today's terms would have exceeded that of John McCormack, Michael Jackson, and U2.

I say this because, as this book and recording try to demonstrate, besides being a distinguished artist, he also had a profound and lasting political influence. Moore wrote and performed at a time when the common English view of the Irish was that they were savages. That, of course, was fundamentally a political stance since, by demeaning the character and culture of the Irish people, it somehow justified dominating them.

The chief importance of Moore is that he both challenged and overcame the prevalent English prejudices towards the Irish. Moreover, he did this on their own turf—that is, within the great drawing rooms of the English aristocracy. How was it possible to dismiss a people who had produced songs which, in their exquisite combination of poetry and music, were on par with the great classical composers of Europe? I use the word *people* advisedly—for, in every thought and action of his life, Moore, with the greatest humility, said that he was merely the artistic vessel through which a culture of great lineage and distinction flowed:

> If the pulse of the patriot, soldier or lover,
> Have throbbed at our lay, 'tis thy glory alone;
> It was but as the wind passing heedlessly over,
> And all the wild sweetness I waked was thy own.

Because he functioned as a political emissary in a foreign land, the message of Moore had to be cloaked in flowery allusion, like that of the *aisling* school of the eighteenth century. Instead, he conjured a vision in which Ireland, in the guise of a woman beset with sorrow, appears to the poet in a half-conscious dream. Moore, a fervent Irish nationalist, could not always speak his mind directly.

As Tim Pat Coogan has said, Moore lived most of his life with his head under the parapet. He could not always name his besetters, and for this he was unfairly mocked. Byron's wisecrack, "Tommy loves a lord," was often quoted by those who should have known better. He depended on the dispensers of patronage for his sustenance, there being little for artists in the poverty-stricken Ireland of his day in which the Act of Union had virtually destroyed the Irish economy. To a sensitive listener and reader, however, there is great principle and courage in Moore—and this is evidenced as much in the sorrow as in the anger expressed in his *Irish Melodies*. Indeed, for Moore, the sorrow and anger came from the same source—a sense of outrage at the great wrong done to his people.

The real importance of Moore is, as I have emphasized, that he envisaged a better future for Ireland even while facing the bitter realities of the present moment. Arguably, without Moore there wouldn't have been a Yeats; and without Yeats there wouldn't have been a *Riverdance* to celebrate all that political and intellectual freedom has brought to the Republic of Ireland.

Another deeply important aspect of Moore is that his understanding of Irishness embraced many diverse viewpoints and traditions. In this he was a living example of ecumenism in action. A Catholic by birth, he fought for the rights of his co-religionists. Yet he married a Protestant and was equally careful to see that the rights and traditions of Protestants were also recognized and respected. He was, of course, a follower of the United Irishmen—the only major political movement in Irish history in which Protestants of the North came together with Catholics for the larger good of Ireland as a whole. Moore's understanding of a United Ireland still stands as an example to those who would brand anyone who does not share their political and religious views as "un-Irish." These narrow-minded attitudes also extend to class prejudices in which art songs like those of Moore are dismissed merely because they were sung in middle-class drawing rooms. A strange reaction, that! In my own childhood, Moore's *Melodies* sat on our family piano and served to inculcate a great pride in our Irish heritage.

Tom Moore paved the way for a cultural movement that today has won global recognition. That movement was predicated upon the hard-won freedoms advanced by Moore. Given his pluralistic philosophy and ecumenical spirit, no major intellectual and artistic figure of the past, other than Yeats, is more in tune with a future Ireland than Moore, whose life and art are a celebration of all that is best in the Irish tradition.

James W. Flannery
Atlanta
September 1997

Bibliography

Osborn Bergin. *Irish Bardic Poetry* (Dublin: The Dublin Institute for Advanced Studies, 1970).

Margery Brady. *The Last Rose of Summer: The Love Story of Tom Moore and Bessy Dyke* (Kilkenny: Greens Hill Publications, 1993).

Brendán Brenthnach. *Folk Music and Dances of Ireland* (Dublin: Mercier Press, 1977).

Charlotte Brooke. *Reliques of Irish Poetry* (Gainesville, Florida: Scholars' Facsimiles and Reprints, 1970). Introduction by Leonard R. N. Ashley.

Edward Bunting, ed. *The Ancient Music of Ireland* (Dublin: Waltons, 1969). Contains Bunting collections and critical notes of 1796, 1809 and 1840.

Seamus Deane. *Celtic Revivals* (Winston-Salem: Wake Forest Press, 1985).

———, general ed. *The Field Day Anthology of Irish Writing* (Derry: Field Day Publications, 1991). Volume 1.

Miriam Allen deFord. *Thomas Moore* (New York: Twayne Publishers, Inc., 1967).

Denis Donoghue. *We Irish* (New York: Alfred A. Knopf, 1986).

Wilfred S. Dowden, ed. *The Letters of Thomas Moore* (Oxford: Oxford University Press, 1964). Two volumes.

Terry Eagleton. *Heathcliff and the Great Hunger* (London: Verso, 1995).

Terry Eagleton et al. *Nationalism, Colonialism and Literature* (Minneapolis: University of Minnesota Press, 1990).

R. F. Foster. *Modern Ireland 1600–1972* (London: Allen Lane, 1988).

———. *Paddy and Mr. Punch: Connections in Irish and English History* (London: Allen Lane, 1993).

Marilyn Gaull. *English Romanticism: The Human Context* (New York: Norton, 1988).

John Hutchinson. *The Dynamics of Cultural Nationalism* (London: Allen & Unwin, 1987).

Robert Kee. *Ireland, A History* (London: Sphere Books, 1982).

Ernest J. Lovell, Jr., ed. *Lady Blessington's Conversations of Lord Byron* (Princeton: Princeton University Press, 1969).

Leslie Marchand, ed. *Lord Byron: Selected Letters and Journals* (Cambridge, Massachusetts: Harvard University Press, 1973).

Thomas Moore. *The Irish Melodies* (London: Boosey & Co., 1895). Arranged by Charles Villiers Stanford.

————. *Memoirs of Captain Rock, the Celebrated Irish Chieftain* (New York: J. McLoughlin, 1824).

————. *The Poetical Works of Thomas Moore* (New York: D. Appleton & Co., 1856).

————. *Travels of an Irish Gentleman* (London: Charles Dolman, 1853).

Howard Mumford Jones. *The Harp That Once: A Chronicle of the Life of Thomas Moore* (New York: Holt and Co., 1937).

Sean O'Boyle. *The Irish Song Tradition* (Dublin: Gilbert Dalton, 1976).

Tomas O'Canainn. *Traditional Music in Ireland* (London: Routledge and Kegan Paul, 1978).

David O'Connell. *The Irish Roots of Margaret Mitchell's Gone With the Wind* (Decatur, Georgia: Claves & Petry, Ltd., 1996).

Frank O'Connor. *The Backward Look: A Survey of Irish Literature* (London: Macmillan, 1967).

Sylvester O'Halloran. *An Introduction to the Study of the History and Antiquities of Ireland* (Dublin: Thomas Ewing, 1772).

Donald O'Sullivan. *Carolan: The Life, Times and Music of an Irish Harper* (Routledge and Kegan Paul Ltd., 1958). Two volumes.

————. *Songs of the Irish* (Dublin: Browne and Nolan, 1960).

Peter Quennell, ed. *Genius in the Drawing Room: The Literary Salon in the Nineteenth and Twentieth Centuries* (London: Weidenfeld & Nicolson, 1980).

Joan Rimmer. *The Irish Harp* (Cork: Mercier Press, 1984).

Charles Rosen. *The Classical Style: Haydn, Mozart, Beethoven* (New York: Norton, 1972).

————. *The Romantic Generation* (Cambridge, Massachusetts: Harvard University Press, 1995).

William Sharp, ed. *The Poems of Ossian* (Edinburgh: John Grant, 1926). Translated by James Macpherson.

L. A. G. Strong. *The Minstrel Boy* (London: Hodder and Stoughton, 1937).

Thérèse Tessier. *The Bard of Erin: A Study of Thomas Moore* (Salzburg: Institut für Anglistik und Amerikanstik, 1981).

Mary Helen Thuente. *The Harp Restrung: The United Irishmen and the Rise of Irish Literary Nationalism* (New York: Syracuse University Press, 1994).

Michael R. Turner, ed. *The Parlour Song Book* (New York: The Viking Press, 1972).

Norman Vance. *Irish Literature: A Social History* (Oxford: Blackwell, 1990).

Terence de Vere White. *Tom Moore: The Irish Poet* (London: Hamish Hamilton, 1977).

Sources of Illustrations

The author and publisher would like to thank the individuals and institutions listed below for kindly granting permission to reproduce the photographs and illustrations included in this book.

Emory University: author photo
Seamus Heaney (photography by Roy Hewson): p. 12
Manchester City Art Galleries: p. 60
National Gallery of Ireland: front cover, pp. 2, 17, 36, 38, 47, 58, 65, 72, 75, 99, 113, 114, 155
Royal Irish Academy (photography by Sean Kennedy, The Green Studio): pp. 62, 77, 122, 137, 146, 162
Trinity College, Dublin (photography by Sean Kennedy, The Green Studio): pp. 40, 48

About the Artists

JAMES W. FLANNERY is the son of Irish emigrants, James and Nellie Cotter Flannery, who settled in Hartford, Connecticut. He holds a B.A. from Trinity College, Hartford, an M.F.A. from the Yale School of Drama and a Ph.D. from Trinity College, Dublin. A specialist in the dramatic work of William Butler Yeats, Mr. Flannery founded the Yeats International Theatre Festival at Dublin's Abbey Theatre in 1989, and was executive director of the Festival from 1989 to 1993. He is the author of the definitive study *W. B. Yeats and the Idea of a Theatre: The Early Abbey Theatre in Theory and Practice* (Yale, 1976, 1989).

As a singer, Mr. Flannery has concertized widely in the United States, Canada and Europe, most recently at the residence of Jean Kennedy Smith, U.S. ambassador to Ireland, in the summer of 1997. In 1993 he received the prestigious Wild Geese Award for Outstanding Contribution to Irish Culture, and has been honored among the "one hundred most prominent Irish Americans" by *Irish America* magazine on several occasions. He lives in Atlanta, Georgia, and teaches at Emory University.

JANET HARBISON is one of Ireland's most accomplished harpers as well as a distinguished ethnomusicologist and composer. As a harper, she has performed on a wide variety of concert platforms, from the Royal Festival Hall in London to the village stage of Ballyporeen, County Tipperary, for President Reagan's visit to his ancestral home. As a composer, Ms. Harbison has numerous choral works, film scores, and recordings to her credit, including a solo collection, *O'Neill's Harper*. In 1992 she founded the Belfast Harp Orchestra, which achieved international acclaim for its Grammy Award–winning album with the Chieftains, *The Celtic Harp*.